Love,
Teach

Love, Teach

REAL STORIES AND HONEST
ADVICE TO KEEP TEACHERS FROM
CRYING UNDER THEIR DESKS

Kelly Treleaven

Avery
an imprint of Penguin Random House
New York

AVERY

an imprint of Penguin Random House LLC

penguinrandomhouse.com

Most Avery books are available at special quantity discounts for bulk purchase for sales promotions, premiums, fund-raising, and educational needs. Special books or book excerpts also can be created to fit specific needs. For details, write SpecialMarkets@ penguinrandomhouse.com.

Library of Congress Cataloging-in-Publication Data

Names: Treleaven, Kelly, author.

Title: Love, teach : real stories and honest advice to keep teachers from crying under their desks / Kelly Treleaven.

Description: New York : Avery, an imprint of Penguin Random House LLC, 2020. | Includes bibliographical references.

Identifiers: LCCN 2019057938 (print) | LCCN 2019057939 (ebook) | ISBN 9780593190319 (paperback) | ISBN 9780525533160 (ebook)

Subjects: LCSH: First year teachers—Handbooks, manuals, etc.

Classification: LCC LB2844.1.N4 T74 2020 (print) | LCC LB2844.1.N4 (ebook) | DDC 371.102—dc23

LC record available at https://lccn.loc.gov/2019057938

LC ebook record available at https://lccn.loc.gov/2019057939

p. cm.

Printed in the United States of America

10 9 8 7 6 5 4 3 2 1

Book design by Shannon Plunkett

For Don and Jean Treleaven, my first teachers

Author's Note

Human memory is highly flawed, especially when that human is experiencing the emotional turbulence that is the first few years of teaching. I have tried to re-create conversations and events to the best of my ability. Though all stories are as true as I remember them to be, certain names and identifying details have been changed to protect the privacy of individuals.

Additionally, all of the views and opinions in this book—on teaching, interpersonal relationships, superior Pop-Tart flavors, etc.—are my own and not the views of my employer.

Contents

Introduction

One of my worst days of teaching happened on a day I wasn't even there.

The Day the Wall Came Off, as I would later call it, was the day my substitute teacher failed to show up for my last-period English class full of eighth graders. During that time, students in my class:

- Duct-taped one another to their chairs and the wall,
- Destroyed and wrote crude messages on absent students' property,
- Had a "snowball fight," which consisted of crumpling up all the paper they could find and throwing it at one another,
- Threatened students who tried to leave to go get help, and
- Left all their trash on the floor when the bell rang, which was so abundant that it almost covered the floor.

How did I learn all of this if I wasn't there, you ask? I saw it. A student in my class posted a video of the mayhem on Facebook, and word eventually got around to another teacher who called me after school.

I was embarrassed, of course, but more than anything, I was hurt. Like many end-of-the-day classes, my seventh period was a little rowdier, but I loved them. I let their jokes run a little longer than they needed to and planned way more out-of-your-seat activities, and in exchange they let me have the floor when I needed it. They were not a perfect class by any stretch, but by now, in March, I would never have believed they would do something like this.

This was about me, obviously.[1] Any respect I'd thought my students had for me was a complete illusion. Just when I thought teaching was getting easier, just when I thought I might have this thing under control, I learned that I was a failure.

I returned to school the next day with a plan. When my students walked in and took their seats, heads bowed in contrition, I knew they realized that I had heard about what had happened the day before. Usually rambunctious, my eighth graders were silent. First, I passed out a piece of paper to each student and I asked them to write down exactly what happened and why none of them did the right thing and got another teacher.

Then I did something that still makes me cringe.

I held up a medium-sized cardboard box. Earlier in the day I had emptied the hole punch cartridge of all three copy machines in the school and ripped up paper scraps I'd found in the recycling bin until I had a layer several inches thick of confetti paper.

I explained that I'd seen a video of their antics and the mess left in my classroom. "This box doesn't have close to the amount of trash I saw in the video," I began. "And for that, you're lucky. But I want you to spend the last few minutes of class experiencing what it was like for someone else to have to pick up after you and the 'fun' you had yesterday."

Students gawked as I shook out the box evenly around the

---

1   (It was not, but more on that later.)

room, making sure not to deposit too much in any one place. I wasn't about to make it easy for them.

"Not a single person leaves this class until every last one of these pieces of paper is back in the box. If I see you talking, being silly, or not helping pick up, you will clean up this whole box by yourself tomorrow during lunch."

Everyone hopped out of their seat and began silently collecting paper. The few times that a student whispered or giggled, nearby students would whip their heads around, shushing them aggressively.

Eventually, after they scooped up all the paper, I had the students sit back in their desks quietly until the bell rang.

When the last student left, I went over to my desk and slumped in my chair. Stupidly, I had thought that forcing my students to march through this parade of shame might make me feel better, but I felt exactly as mad as I had before class started, maybe even more. The whole event—from my students' misbehavior to my response to it—felt like a defeat. I couldn't help but think that this entire situation would never have happened to a better teacher, and if it did, a truly good teacher would have dealt with it more wisely than I did. I knew I shouldn't have used a group punishment for the wrongs of a few. I should have engaged the class in dialogue to talk calmly about why this happened, who it affected, and how we can improve instead of resorting to a belittling reprimand. But I hadn't done any of that. *What is wrong with you? Ms. Jimenez would never have done something like this,*[2] I thought to myself. I was frustrated, and I was ashamed.

I glanced over at the stacks of paper I'd made students write

---

2   Ms. Jimenez is a fabulous science teacher who taught down the hall from me at the time.

to me about what had happened the day before and pulled them toward me. Some letters made me laugh.

I was asleep most of the time, but I did hear yelling.

*When we came in the classroom we saw there was no sub,
so we sat down for a minute. Then it got boring,
so we started to tape people in chairs.*

*I had told the others to stop what they were doing but they
wouldn't stop. I didn't even see the wall come off.*

I quickly checked the room, expecting to see a hole in the wall I'd missed or chipped paint from some kind of destruction but couldn't find anything. Eventually, I came to the conclusion that this student must have meant it metaphorically, which, when I thought about moments of chaos from my own life, I understood perfectly.

Other letters made me cry.

I know you are disappointed in me because you trusted me a lot.

*You do get a "sorry" from me. I am sorry for looking
at all that and doing nothing.*

We disappointed you and it hurt.

*I didn't do the right thing. It felt like I couldn't but
I know I could have.*

*Even if you don't want to accept my apology,
I am still very sorry.*

I put my head in my hands. Deep down I knew I wasn't actually mad at my students. I was mad about something much larger and more complicated and far more devastating than a messy classroom. It even went beyond the feeling of being disrespected, though that certainly stung. It was the frustration of knowing my students deserved better—that, because of their zip code, they had to go to the type of school where substitutes just didn't show up and where the lack of funding meant I had to shoulder student discipline. Even though I was working as hard as I knew how, I had still let them down.

But I lived through The Day the Wall Came Off. Here is a short list of some things I've learned since:

- Never equate the behavior of your students with your worth as a teacher.
- Developing a relationship with your students that makes them feel heard and valued is critical in teaching *and* classroom management.
- Don't listen to the mean voice in your head that wants to say you are a failure of a teacher.
- Never, ever compare yourself to Ms. Jimenez (or whatever superstar teacher is down the hall).
- The bad days pass and the small victories make a difference.

I had to spend years in the classroom to learn those essential truths about teaching. But I want to share this wisdom—and more—with you in this book to give you essential perspective from the trenches, whether you are considering a career in teaching, have just started, or have been teaching for years.

This book was born out of bad days, days when I was sure I was alone. But it was also born out of love—for my students, for education, for teachers everywhere, and for the younger teacher I once was, sitting at my desk at the end of that day back in March 2012 with my head in my hands.

Lastly, this book is inspired by the apology and the promise I gave to my students two days after The Day the Wall Came Off. I told them they were good kids, and good kids mess up sometimes. I told them that teachers mess up sometimes, too, and that I had really, really messed up. I told them that failure isn't making mistakes but refusing to do better. I promised to do better.

I would have other bad days in the future. I would have days that ended with me sobbing in my car, days when I would go home and browse career sites and fall asleep before dinner, days when it felt like the walls not only came off but completely disintegrated.

Even so, I have kept my promise to them.

For them, I've done better.

I arrived at teaching via a detour. Education had not been on my radar at all when I was initially considering career options. A voracious reader since childhood, I had planned my life and college courses around going into publishing. But, after graduating in 2009, I found myself with an English degree, no internship experience (four of the five internships I'd applied to completely canceled their internship programs, still recovering from the recession), and the growing realization that I was unemployed. "You can always teach," my parents told me while I cried on their couch one day.

The more I thought about it, the more I considered the possibility that I might really enjoy teaching. After all, I had always loved learning and being a student. I loved reading and talking about books with people. I cared a lot about what I knew of inequity. I loved kids. I was creative. I was a hard worker. Wasn't that what a good teacher should be?

And so I enrolled in what was, at the time, one of Houston's top alternative certification programs. I spent a year getting certified, substituting when I wasn't in class or student teaching. In the fall of 2010, I started out in a classroom of my own.

To say I was unprepared is like saying that a baby is unprepared to fly a plane. I quickly realized that very little of the advice I'd read in my teaching courses was relevant or applicable in a real-life classroom, and that even my student teaching and the role-play scenarios were nothing like being a teacher on my own. I also discovered that the other new teachers around me felt the same way, whether they had done a six-week training with a popular teaching placement program or had gotten their bachelor's in education at a four-year college. I knew I had found myself on a bizarre, wild, and demanding journey, and I had no idea what my destination was even supposed to look like.

A few weeks into my first year I began blogging anonymously under the pseudonym "Love, Teach"—the way I would sign off on my blog posts—as a way to keep my family and friends updated on my teaching journey without having to repeat my sob stories of failure over and over. (I did a lot of crying in those rookie years.) Within a few years, *Love, Teach* grew from a handful of readers to thousands. It was clear that the frustrations I was experiencing as a new teacher combined with the fierce loyalty I felt for my students was a feeling not limited to my school, to Houston, to Texas, or even to America.

Though I continued to struggle, I took comfort in knowing that at least I wasn't alone.

I'm a big believer in the detour—the idea that even if there is an impassable roadblock in the path we originally planned on taking, there is something ultimately beautiful and necessary in the alternate route. These alternate routes can be rougher and take longer, but it's on the road less traveled that we often encounter the limits of ourselves, the extraordinary, the divine.

Though teaching was my detour, it's been one of the most important journeys I've ever found myself on. My natural tendency is to be anxious or skeptical about almost everything, but with teaching, I know with a permeating sense of certainty that I am doing exactly what I'm supposed to be doing right now. Even when teaching was the hardest and when I seriously doubted my own effectiveness, I had a profound sense that the work of teachers matters deeply. Not a lot of people have that kind of clarity of purpose about what they do, and I am grateful for it.

Being a teacher has changed me. It has broken me, but it has also rebuilt me into something stronger and kinder, both gentler and more badass. Teaching has ramped up my anxiety to near-crippling levels at times, but it has also forced me to have more respect for myself than I've ever had before. It has given me access to a world that I can't imagine not having citizenship in, a place where I have the honor of standing beside other humans as they use their own voices and the stories of others to build a better world. Teaching has made me more open-minded, more aware of my biases, more grateful, more connected to the world around me, than I have ever been before. For me, it is a way to impact our world for the better at a time when there's so much chaos and disillusionment surrounding us. As a friend recently told me, "What a blessing, to model a better world every day for young people." And it is. Even on the very worst and darkest days, it is.

As of this writing, I've just started my tenth year of teaching. For the first five years I taught in Title I schools, and I currently teach in a public charter school created by my district to meet the needs of highly gifted children. I've taught fourth grade to ninth grade, from English to English as a Second Language to social studies, but the bulk of my experience has been as a middle school English teacher. I've taught children with dual-exceptionalities, students with Oppositional Defiant Disorder (ODD), and children with both. I've lost sleep worrying about children many people would assume have nothing but also about children many people would expect to have everything. I say this because there is a wide spectrum of experiences in the teaching world, and I think it's important for anyone who writes about teaching to know more than one student population.

That being said, ten years of experience doesn't make me an expert. I'm not a consultant or a doctor or a "thought leader." I've never posted an inspirational education meme with a beach background on Twitter, and I hope I never will. I'm a teacher and I write about it. I'm still learning. We all are.

If you're looking for a textbook, an exhaustive reference book, or even a strictly professional resource, I sincerely urge you to look elsewhere. In fact, I submitted an early version of this book to a group that only publishes professional development educational texts and resources, and they told me they loved it, but there were *too many stories*. Let that be a warning to you.

This is, however, the book that I needed as a new teacher. In the years when I struggled the most, I needed the voice of someone who had been there. Not "been there" thirty years ago— before e-mail, online gradebooks, and social media. Not "been there" as in the teacher had only worked in well-funded schools with essentially unlimited resources. I wanted to read advice from someone who had been in a school like mine recently. Someone who had truly walked in my shoes.

I also did not want sugarcoated narratives or inspirational tweets that suggest a positive attitude or "remembering your why"[3] are solutions for any teaching challenge. The truth is much messier: Sometimes being a teacher means finally getting through to that difficult student, and sometimes it means crying in the shower because you are not sure you can physically make it to winter break. Teachers need to be reassured that other teachers struggle, they fail, and they get back up again.

The fight for public education is tough—and not in the teacher-hero way that Hollywood likes to portray (cue the minute-long montage set to inspirational music of a determined, attractive teacher grading in her classroom as the sun goes down). It's tough in a way that can be dark and jarring and shameful. I've had eighth graders in my class who were *functionally illiterate*, and I've gone to my principal or other staff for help only to be met with some version of "There are twenty-nine other students in that class that need you" or "Sadly, we have more serious things to worry about right now" or "Welcome to public education."

Some may find it disheartening to read about how hard this profession can be, but I don't mean to discourage you in any way. There's power in sharing our experiences, in supporting one another through something as important as education in America. Our passion gives us a common goal. And for most

---

3 Remembering your "why" (why you became a teacher) is a good practice, but for new, overwhelmed teachers it's about as helpful as applying topical muscle cream to a leg with a broken femur.

teachers, our hurt and frustration comes from the fact that we love this job deeply and fiercely.

I also think that it's important to speak about teaching in an unfiltered, honest way. We will never improve the system for teachers or students in this country if we do not use our voices to call out problems in education today. That's part of our job and our responsibility to our kids.

This book may make you laugh, and it might also make you cry, but my hope is that if you're a new teacher you'll find the support and guidance I wish I'd had. And if you are about to embark on a teaching career—if you're reading this in the summer before your first year or during your teacher training, know this: Education is hard and will demand everything you have, but it's the most important job in the world. I believe that with my whole heart and I will never stop fighting for it.

I hope you'll join me.

We need you.

Part I

Before
You Start

CHAPTER 1

Choosing a District and a School

I joke sometimes that I knew nothing about being teacher until I became one. But I knew a few things.

First, I knew why I wanted to be a teacher—I love kids, I'm a hard worker, I believe in giving back, and I value so many of my own teachers and the impact they had on me. I was also certain I wanted to teach English because I love anything involving words: whether it's writing them, reading them, talking about them, or getting other people excited about them. I also knew the textbook version of *how* to teach from my pedagogy courses, a good chunk of which I would discover wasn't relevant to my situation when I was faced with real life.

I knew that I didn't want to teach kids whose GPAs or AP test scores I could possibly mess up by not being a great teacher yet, and I also knew I didn't want to teach kids who were still losing teeth.[1] I knew I wanted to teach in a low-income school because I cared about the achievement gap and because I'd seen the

---

1   Joke's on me as I quickly discovered there are middle schoolers who are STILL LOSING TEETH!

movie *Freedom Writers,* which at the time seemed like all the qual-
ification I needed to teach in areas affected by poverty, systemic
racism, and other forces I'd never encountered in my privileged
existence. (Note: *It is not.*)

But beyond that, I hadn't given much thought to where I
wanted to teach. My main criteria for choosing a school and district was any school that would hire me.

So, when it came time for me to choose a school, I went to a
job fair for the largest district in the city almost completely unprepared. I knew this district had the type of schools I wanted to
work in, but I had little to no knowledge of the operations in
that district, its board of trustees, or its reputation. I wandered
from table to table, eventually finding an assistant principal of a
middle school who admitted he had just found out about the
job fair an hour earlier and had a very scattered understanding
of the openings in his school ("I'm pretty sure you could have
your pick of grade level—I know we have a *lot* of openings in
English"). I arranged an interview with him—with one school
only—left the job fair, and accepted an offer from that school
three days later.

Luckily for me, my somewhat reckless approach to choosing
a district and school led to many positive outcomes.

First of all, I'm so glad I chose middle school. Even though
my students drive me to the edge of insanity sometimes, they are
also, year after year, the best people I know. I read this quote
about teenagers recently on Twitter and wished I could retweet
it a thousand times:

> I am a better person for being around teenagers . . . not
> because they test me, but because they have this perfect
> balance of unapologetic and fiery strength and unfiltered,

raw vulnerability. They are beautiful examples of aliveness.

We should all strive for a little more of that.

—Amy Fast, Ed. D (@fastcrayon)

Teenagers forever. Amen.

I'm glad I blindly picked a district; it's allowed me to see and shed light on the tragedy of what happens to students in schools run under ineffective leadership at multiple levels. I don't know if I would have seen that degree of poor leadership had I started at a smaller district where powers are better checked and monitored.

If you aren't sure what kind of environment would be the best fit and want to use my approach to picking a district and school, by all means, go for it. I'm convinced that I had specific things to learn in the places I ended up, even if the way I ended up there seemed random. If you're reading this and are already in a set teaching position or find yourself in a time crunch where you kind of have to go with your first offer, don't worry: *There's no reason you can't have a great teaching experience wherever you are.*

But.

If I had the chance to do the entire process over again, I can't say that I would do it in the exact same way. This chapter has some guidance I'd follow if I found myself starting from the beginning again.

MAKING INFORMED CHOICES FOR YOURSELF

When you really look at it, the number of decisions that brand-new teachers have to make before even interviewing for a position is kind of insane. After choosing a state and a district—which are big choices themselves—there are endless things to consider:

Small school or large school?

Middle or high school?

Kindergarten or fifth grade?

Public or private?

Urban or rural?

Title I [2] or non–Title I?

Each of these decisions has a number of implications. Choose a small school and you may love the familial nature of the faculty, or you may feel as if you and your work are under a microscope. Choose a large school and you may be energized by the wide range of teachers and students to connect with, or you may be disappointed by the anonymity you experience. Teachers in Title I schools are often passionate about the urgency of their mission, but it can be hard to practice self-care with the workload and emotional weight that comes with teaching in a community affected by poverty. On the other end, teachers in wealthier schools may enjoy better resources and facilities but feel weighed down by bureaucratic pressures or constant parent interference. Perks and pitfalls come with all of these options, but the key is finding the right fit for *you*.

Unless you're in some kind of fellowship or program assigning you to a school, you will have agency in where you choose to interview. But once you're in a school, you may not get your top choice for grade level or content. Your school might even change the grade level you're teaching the week before school starts (speaking from experience here). The administrative decisions about your position or scheduling can have a big impact on what your teaching looks like. Any elementary teacher will tell you that kindergarten and fifth grade are in completely

---

2   This is a term for schools that receive federal funding because they have higher concentrations of students from lower-income homes.

different universes. Secondary teachers will tell you about how wonderful or terrible they think being on block schedule is or how different their freshmen class is from their senior class. Teachers who have taught in more than one school or in more than one district can rattle off the differences—good and bad—between their experiences, from central administration all the way down to the online grading portal or substitute system.

The bad news is that it's almost impossible to know what your exact experience will be like until you arrive at your school, roll up your sleeves, and start teaching.

The good news is that there are easy, manageable things you can do to give yourself an *idea* of what that particular sort of teaching job may be like. Even if you don't have much of a choice in the school that hires you, there is plenty you can do to prepare ahead of time for your role. This doesn't mean you won't have a learning curve, but you'll at least have the knowledge that *certain things are going to be on your learning curve*. It's like looking up the traffic report on your phone before leaving for a meeting. If you head out the door twenty minutes earlier it doesn't mean you won't have to sit in traffic or that you're guaranteed no accidents. It just means you have a better chance of calmly arriving on time and, in my case, ideally with an iced coffee, instead of sprinting in at the last minute, sweaty, uncaffeinated, and apologizing.[3] If I had done my research, I may have still made many of the decisions I did but with better information allowing me to anticipate and plan for many of the challenges I found in my first few years of teaching.

---

3 I'm referring to Houston traffic, Houston heat, and my own crippling fear of being late and/or sweaty at meetings here.

Here's some specific advice on making informed choices when it comes to choosing where to teach:

Observe a Wide Range of Teachers and Schools Before Making a Decision

During my certification, I observed a brand-new teacher in a high school classroom in a wealthy suburban district and several veteran teachers in a Title I private charter school. The Title I school had an effective school-wide discipline policy while the wealthy school did not, so when I saw quiet, compliant classes at the Title I school and unruly, chaotic classes walking all over the newbie teacher at the wealthy school, I walked away from those experiences thinking that teaching Title I would be easy and that teaching in wealthier areas would be difficult. I made huge, vaulting leaps to a conclusion based on minimal information.

The number of hours I spent in these classrooms met the requirements for my teaching certification program, but I wish I would have spent way more time observing a wider range of classrooms. It would have been helpful to watch, say, a middle school classroom in a school similar to one you want to work in, or one of the best high school English teachers in a district, or a new teacher with a significant ESL population—areas you may not have gained experience with in your student teaching. These opportunities are available if you ask, and they're completely worth the time and extra bit of effort if they help you make a more informed decision about where you want to teach.

Another point: Many certification programs have their teacher candidates conduct observations before their student teaching placement, and while I see the usefulness of doing it in this order, definitely take opportunities to observe teachers *after* your student teaching placement if you can. Once you've started teaching, you'll be better able to interpret what you are observing and what to look for.

Ask teachers in the area about various districts and schools' reputations. Chances are, you already have an idea of what type of school you want to work in, and most local teachers will either be able to give you some recommendations about the reputations of schools and districts OR refer you to someone who has better information than they do. Leadership can truly make or break a school experience. Remember to take everyone's opinions with a grain of salt; when I told some people at my new job that I came from a particular Title I school in our district—a school I loved and still miss—they grimaced as if I'd said I'd been teaching in an opium den.

If you're moving to a new area where you don't know anyone, try looking up Facebook groups of local teachers/professional organizations and asking if you can meet with a teacher in the area, or even go into a coffee shop for an afternoon and ask a barista to point out any teachers to you. You can even try to identify them yourself. Just look for large totes, flat shoes, bags under their eyes, and pen/dry-erase markers on their forearms.

Do Some Soul-Searching About What Kind of School You Want to Work In and Why

No matter what kind of environment you want to work in, you should take a good look at your intentions, and really examine what you imagine the experience will look like. I came into teaching wanting to work with underprivileged children, and so I was drawn to a Title I school. But though many of my intentions were pure, I can see now that a big part of the narrative I wanted was really about what I could achieve as a teacher and the altruism I envisioned others seeing in me, notions fed by narratives that center around a white "savior" character from movies and literature I loved like *The Blind Side* and *To Kill a Mockingbird.*

What I learned in teaching is that I am not the hero in this story, and that leadership looks way more like serving than it does being a superstar. I learned that you will "save" no one if you believe you're in a superior position to save others in the first place. I learned that in teaching, you won't always get the thank-you note about how you changed a student's life, the weepy Hollywood success story, or adulations from parents. I learned that the leaders I most want to emulate are the ones quietly grabbing a mop in the cafeteria when they see a mess after fifth-grade lunch is dismissed, not the ones posting thank-you letters from students on social media.[4]

If the pictures in your head are more about the adoration or gratitude you will receive—being adored, "saving" children you believe can't save themselves—you may want to spend some time getting your motivations in check before deciding to become a teacher. Your gas tank will be very empty very quickly if recognition or outward validation fuel your teaching.

Educate Yourself on Issues Affecting the Population(s) You Want to Work With

Regardless of where and what age you teach, to be an effective teacher you *must advocate for your students,* and to do that, you need to understand as much about them as you can. Don't wait

---

4   Be careful posting any pictures or student work on social media, but especially an intimate, heartfelt note from a student who wrote it under the assumption that the audience was just you.

until the school year starts to find out about the systems, ideologies, and biases that may be holding your students back. I know that, personally, my limited knowledge of poverty and institutional racism resulted in missed opportunities and harm to my students. It took a long time for me to admit this—I think for many years I preferred to think my good intentions meant I was *doing* good—but I wish I'd done way more to educate myself on poverty and race-related issues than my teaching certification program did before I started teaching.

No matter where you teach, it's critical to have a strong understanding of racial and cultural biases. I believed in the importance of diversity before I started teaching, but I had never really challenged myself on what that means. If I had educated myself just a little bit, I would have seen that I was holding on to the problematic idea that "I don't see color"—something I thought was progressive but actually allowed me to be dismissive of the very real issues my students of color were facing. I would have recognized that I didn't have the diverse curriculum I thought I did and made changes. I would also have been more sensitive in evaluating how I was inadvertently valuing "whiteness" in the way I policed how my students spoke and behaved, such as correcting their pronunciation of words like *asked* being said as *axed*, even in informal dialogue. I would have given my students space to actually talk about the ways that racism and cultural bias affected them instead of limiting their discussions and writing to topics *I* was comfortable with. Some good sites for furthering your education and to help you find resources from experts are tolerance.org and zinnedproject.org. Hashtags like #educolor, #ClearTheAir, and #ClearTheAirEdu are also great starting points for your journey.

Be Flexible, Curious, and Grateful (FCG)

Don't come into teaching with any rigid expectations. Be bendy. Mold-y. Ready to be changed. This is one of my top pieces of advice for new teachers, period, not just when it comes to choosing a school. You will have a much better teaching experience if you hold everything with open hands, ready to grow and learn and embrace rather than trying to control everything or make it fit whatever narrative you had going into teaching. Look at the difference between a first-year teacher with a fixed mind-set and an FCG mind-set.

> **FIXED:** I *have* to get a job at X school. Anything less and I'll be miserable.

> **FCG:** I hope I get a job at X school, but if I don't, I know I'll gain valuable teaching experience anywhere.

> **FIXED:** I'm having such a hard time teaching. This wouldn't happen if I was teaching at X school or had accepted that other position.

> **FCG:** Hoooo, boy. This is rough, but I know that growth is always disruptive. One day I'll be grateful for the learning I did here and how it opened my eyes to ineffective leadership or what happens when states slash education budgets.

> **FIXED:** I was supposed to come in and be an amazing teacher. Because I'm not amazing yet, I must be a failure.

> **FCG:** Let's see, who can I get a margarita with tonight and laugh about the fact that I accidentally said "slimy cock rod" instead of "slimy rock cod" while reading Amy Tan's short

story out loud and never regained the attention of my class?[5] Because even though I died of embarrassment, it was hilarious and margaritas will resurrect me.

And finally, remember you don't need to find your perfect school on your first placement. I don't know anyone personally who found their perfect school on their very first try. I'm sure they're out there, but most teachers I've talked to took several jobs at several different schools before finding a truly good fit. I am very lucky that I feel like I've found my perfect school now, but let me tell you a secret: *I actually do not wish that I'd found my current school on my first interview.*

I grew so much professionally and emotionally by working in schools that were not a good fit. Those tough years have made me a better teacher, a better public education advocate, a better person, really. And if I'm ever an administrator, you can bet I'll be drawing a lot from my experience on how *not* to behave.

But know you can always get out of a bad situation if you are in one. Teachers do not sign lifelong contracts! You can make adjustments—on a yearly basis, if needed—if your placement turns out to not be the best for you.

As I've said, I wouldn't change the path I've taken, but if I'd been more thoughtful at the beginning of my career, I have to admit that I could have been a better teacher to my students much earlier, and certainly more prepared. First of all, I didn't really understand what teaching in a Title I school would be like. Although Title I schools receive federal funding to try to give

---

5   Why, yes, this *did* happen to me.

those students an equal educational opportunity to match their wealthier peers (where the property taxes offer better resources and facilities), the system is flawed; the reality is that the deeply rooted effects of poverty aren't going to be eliminated by more crayons or free lunches. Title I schools need counselors and very small classes. The districts should offer benefits with comprehensive healthcare that cover therapy and wellness treatments for people who work in their schools to be able to take care of themselves. And finally, they need *excellent*—not baseline—pay for teachers and administrators to attract the best of the best.[6] Right now, most Title I schools have none of those crucial tools.

I knew that teaching at a Title I school would be hard, but I didn't understand that it would demand everything I had. I didn't imagine the day when my students watched another student call me a bitch and was still permitted to remain in my class, without any kind of consequence from the office. I knew that I would have to call parents, but I didn't know that a large percentage of the cell numbers for parents listed in the school's database would no longer be in service a few weeks into the school year. I knew that my administrators would have a lot on their plates, but I wasn't prepared when it took the school counselor an entire semester to recognize my e-mails and in-person pleas about the need for a student who couldn't read, speak, or

---

6 To clarify, I'm not suggesting (and would never suggest) that all teachers in Title I schools are underqualified or untalented. Some of the best teachers I know are working in Title I schools and crushing it. What we have is not a teacher problem but a government problem—one I'll return to throughout this book. Here's what's happening: States are responding to their teacher shortages not by making the drastic improvements necessary to improve conditions for their pool of great teachers but by lowering the qualifications to become a teacher. Often, these less-qualified teachers will find jobs at Title I schools, where acquiring a job is less competitive. Trust me, there are amazing teachers and bad apples in both poor and wealthy schools, but at Title I schools, where students are already behind, they can't afford to have an underqualified teacher.

write in English to be in the ESL beginner class. Or that when the counselor finally recognized the seriousness of this error, her response would be, "I know you can't understand this, but we have bigger fish to fry than an ESL student."

I wouldn't trade my experiences and how it has shaped me as a teacher, and a human being, for anything. But I wish someone had told me before I started that it was going to be difficult in ways I couldn't even begin to understand, and just how long my learning curve would be.

I thought I needed to be teaching in a certain kind of school to have a sense of purpose, but now I know that the values I want to impart in the next generation through literature—the importance of listening to others' stories and working with people who are different from us, the call in each of us to create a better and more just world and the potential of our voices to do that—are messages that young people in every school need to hear.

All in all, I could have had a more enjoyable teaching experience earlier in my career. I may have still chosen to teach middle school, but I would have scheduled observations during my certification year at middle schools *and* at high schools so I could have made an informed decision. I would have requested to observe not only the all-star veterans but also a few new teachers, to get a sense of what type of things I could prepare for— classroom management, instruction, class sizes, procedures, and more.

I would have asked these teachers very specific questions, like:

I'm nervous about being able to manage the behavior of students close to my age. Was this a problem when you started teaching?

I really liked the superorganized way that your students passed in homework. How did you implement that?

I loved the program you used to have students edit one another's papers. Is there a particular training you went to or a resource you could direct me toward so I could learn that?

And I would have used these observations and conversations to inform my decision about where and whom to teach. I often wonder how different my rookie years would have been had I approached someone who knew a lot about the school district and said, "I'm interested in working at a Title I middle school. Can you tell me about the support systems in place for new teachers in your district? Is there a particular campus you might recommend?"

I didn't have the wherewithal to dig this deeply, but you can. But at the end of the day, no matter where you decide to teach—or even if that decision is out of your control due to a teaching placement program—I'm excited for the world of knowledge you're about to acquire. Whether you're teaching in Maine or California, with second graders or seventh graders, being an educator will teach you more than you ever thought possible about yourself, kids, and the world you thought you knew.

You may even learn to tolerate (deep breath) loose teeth.

CHAPTER 2

Interviewing

When I sat down to write this chapter, I thought, *I interview pretty well.* Then I remembered:

- The time I was working at a school so steeped in a toxic culture that, halfway through the interview at another school, I realized just how kind the interviewing principal was and how desperate I was to work for him. After several minutes of trying to hold back my tears, I couldn't anymore and burst into sobs. He had to run out to get a box of tissues while I sat with the rest of the interviewing panel as they said nothing and stared a little too hard.

- The interview in which I yawned every twenty seconds or so because I had started taking a medication the day before that made me incredibly drowsy. The yawns weren't the cute, small kind I could stifle, either—they were huge and violent and took over my body. Then, when it dawned on me how absurd I must look as a teacher candidate *yawning uncontrollably* and what a funny story this would be later, I started laughing. For the rest of the interview I was either laughing, yawning, or apologizing for one of the two.

- The time a principal asked me to speak some Spanish in my interview since I'd listed that I minored in it on my résumé. I felt confident in my Spanish at the time, but I had anticipated that a fellow Spanish-speaker might begin a conversation with me a little more organically, like *Entonces, ¿cómo aprendiste español?* For reasons still unknown to me, I remarked in Spanish that parrots are my favorite bird. One of the assistant principals sitting in on the interview looked at me and raised one eyebrow, as if to say: *Are you even from Earth?*

I may have a talent for embarrassing myself in interviews, but I do have this going for me: Two out of the three what-I-thought-were-terrible interviews I listed above resulted in job offers. If you're nervous about interviewing, this should be highly encouraging to you. Which brings me to one of the most important things I've learned: While the on-paper information and the formal interview answers you provide are important, your ability to bring your authentic self to an interview is important, too, if not more important. This is how, despite yawning, laughing, and crying through many of my interviews, apparently I've at least been able to communicate that teaching and kids matter a lot to me, that I'm a hard worker, and that I either know my stuff or am good at teaching myself stuff. "Well. She may be a weirdo, but perhaps our students might learn from this weirdo," I imagine principals saying moments after I leave the room.

By the way, not all my interviews have been so rife with disaster. I feel I must clarify that for credibility.

I get many e-mails from teachers or about-to-be teachers who are nervous about upcoming interviews and want tips on what they should say, do, or wear to land the job. This makes total sense. As teachers, we are inclined to turn chaos into control; interviews feel chaotic because we don't know exactly what's coming. So it's natural to look for ways to control them somehow by preparing to death. But don't worry! I'm here to tell you everything to anticipate so that your interview goes perfectly and you are 100 percent guaranteed the job.

Just kidding.

First of all, I don't think the right mind-set for interviewing is "I have to be ready for whatever comes my way." No matter how much preparation you do, know that *you can't be prepared for everything.* Go to the nearest mirror and repeat after me: "It is fun to know things, but I do not know all things." (Was your nearest mirror in a public place with strangers around you? I hope so.)

As a person who very much enjoys the idea of being prepared for whatever is about to happen—which is the nicer way of admitting I am a Stage Five Control Freak—I will tell you from firsthand experience that teaching is not the arena to assume predictability, even in the interviewing room. Let me give you an example: In an interview a few years ago, a high school English teacher scoffed at me for not having read "Gooseberries," a short story by Anton Chekhov. She rolled her eyes so hard I thought they would fall out of her head. This threw me off so badly that I spent the rest of the interview stammering and distracted, wondering if that short story was somewhere on the school's curriculum website, or if it was something I'd been asked to read in preparation for the interview (it wasn't). If I had gone into the interview ready for the possibility of being thrown off and accepted that I just might not know all the answers, I might have responded calmly and said, "I haven't, but I'm curious—what about that story in particular do you recommend for teaching?"[1] We'll talk later in this chapter about how to delicately handle questions you don't know how to answer or that may reveal gaps in your knowledge.

Second, I think it's important to think about an interview as a conversation rather than a competition to win. While, yes, the end goal is getting a job and being employed, if we focus too much on "winning," we can make ourselves blind to a lot of important information in the interview: job requirements that weren't in the original posting, red flags about the interviewer's leadership style or communication, opportunities for insight into the way the school is run. In one of my first interviews, I was so focused on doing whatever I needed to present myself as the best candidate that I completely ignored how the principal was treating her secretary (like a child), the types of questions she was asking me (who designed my résumé instead of questions about teaching), and that she might not always have her teachers' interests in mind (she groaned dramatically when I said I might need a few days to think about an offer). The interview should be about both of you putting your best foot forward, and it's a lot easier to listen and observe when you're relaxed.

This isn't to say that you shouldn't prepare at all for your interview and walk in wearing an oversized T-shirt you got for free in college, picking cereal out of your teeth.[2]

Be somewhere in the middle. Here's what I'd recommend:

---

1 Or, if I were a few degrees sassier, I might have said, "Oh, isn't that story the basis for Nadia Kowalski's "Moosedroppings'?"and she would have said, "Why, yes, of course." And I would have said, "Ha! No, it isn't, because I just made up that short story AND that author. Now who looks ridiculous?"

2 Me, right now, at this moment.

1. **Practice responding to the kind of questions you can expect in the interview.** Chances are your teaching certification gave you some idea of the type of questions you'll be asked: Why do you want to be a teacher? What's your teaching philosophy like? How do you plan to communicate with parents? But here are some additional questions from the *Love, Teach* community that would be excellent to help practice interviewing:

Experience

~ What has been the most defining moment in your teaching education/career?

~ What's the most challenging piece of feedback you've received? How did you respond?

Passion and Curiosity

~ What has caught your attention in [relevant field] recently? How do you stay current with your field?

~ What do you know about our school?

~ If you could create your dream classroom, what routines or protocols would you use daily? Weekly?

~ What is your favorite part about [age range of students you'll be teaching]? What are some of the challenges of meeting the needs of [that age range]?

~ In what area of teaching are you most excited to develop professionally?

Instruction

~ If I walk into your classroom, what would I see and hear? What are you doing and what are your students doing?

~ How would you differentiate your instruction for ELL (English Language Learner) students? (Consider the same question for students with disabilities, gifted/talented students, and other groups.)

~ If you give a test and half the class fails it, what do you do?

Relationships/Classroom Management

~ Think of the most challenging student you had during student teaching. What three adjectives would that student use to describe you?

~ How do you build a classroom environment that makes all students feel welcome and wanted?

~ What are your best strategies for building strong relationships with all students?

~ How do you plan to build relationships with parents, families, and the community?

Advocacy

~ What would you do in your classroom to help with your students' mental health and/or social-emotional education?

~ How do you check your own implicit biases when teaching?

~ Explain the difference between equity and equality in teaching.

~ Explain how you will make sure your classroom is culturally responsive.

General

~ Besides teaching, what else does a good teacher do?

~ What is your greatest nonschool-, nonwork-related accomplishment?

~ What is your favorite book?

~ How will you handle bad teaching days?

~ Who is your role model?

~ How will our school be better by hiring you?

My biggest tip for answering any of these is to not think about what the "right answer" is, but to think about what you know to be true about yourself and combine that with what your audience is really looking for by asking that question. For instance, if an interviewer asks, "How will you handle bad teaching days?" you might feel that all you can say is "I don't know" if you haven't started teaching yet. But you *have* had bad days before—think of how you've typically handled those in the past. Then think about what your interviewer is looking for with that question. They want a teacher who is going to stick it out when things get tough and find creative solutions when they're available, not a teacher who will shift the blame to someone else. This can lead you to an answer like, "Well, I haven't started teaching yet, but when I've had bad days in my other jobs, I start by analyzing why I had a bad day to see which parts were under my control. I can see myself as a teacher who looks at bad days and first tries to figure out where things went wrong, then analyzes what I can do about them and searches for solutions."

It's also important to practice your answers out loud. If you can, find an experienced teacher who can do a practice interview with you—asking you questions, listening to your answers, asking follow-up questions you might not have anticipated, and giving you feedback.

2. **Do a full-on investigation of the district and school you're applying to work for.** You want to show your employer that you're not just out there looking for *any* job; you're looking for

their job. Don't be afraid to call or even go in person to check on the status of your application—this shows you're serious. Look on the school or district websites for "About Us" or "Mission" sections, check out their social media feed, know their demographics and school profile. If the website says the school is big on restorative justice circles or a certain writing workshop model, make sure you know what those are and have questions ready about them. Think about how different the interview responses would be from a candidate who did no research on the school compared to you, who knows her stuff.

PRINCIPAL: Why are you a good candidate to work at our school in particular?

NO-RESEARCH CANDIDATE: Well, I'm very passionate about teaching and I love kids.

PRINCIPAL: But why *this* school?

NO-RESEARCH CANDIDATE: Uh . . . I really, really love kids.

PRINCIPAL: So, do you have any more questions?

NO-RESEARCH CANDIDATE: Nope!

PRINCIPAL: Why are you a good candidate to work at our school in particular?

YOU: Well, in looking at the information about your school online, one of the things that immediately attracted me was how much the school has improved in state rankings over the past two years. To me, that's a sign of a campus that is working together on behalf of its students. I also noticed that your school demographics include a high ESL population, and while

I'm not currently ESL certified, I'm already registered to take the certification test in October. Also, I saw on your school's athletic website that you don't have a girls' soccer team—if you need a coach, I'm completely interested.

PRINCIPAL: So, do you have any more questions?

YOU: I saw on the English department website that eighth graders read *I Am Malala* and *A Long Way Gone.* I love those books. Do you happen to know if they read them in literature circles or as whole-class novels? And is there any room for cross-curricular study pairing with the social studies department?

PRINCIPAL (*presses speed dial for HR and whispers into the receiver*): Yes, hi, I'd like to call dibs on an interviewee.

Knowing about the school you're interviewing for doesn't just communicate that you respect the time and workplace of your interviewer—it's also crucial in showing this person that you're smart enough to find information on your own and willing to work hard for things that matter to you. That's a lot of what teaching is, my friends.

3. **Be prepared to not know the answers.** As I touched on earlier, you will inevitably come across something in one of your interviews—a writing method, a technology app, a conference— that you have never heard of. One of the best things you can do is have a good response for when you don't have the right response. Instead of just saying "I don't know," show your enthusiasm and willingness to learn by saying something like:

> "I haven't come across that before. What did you say the name of it was? I'd like to write that down and look into it."

"I haven't personally been trained in that method, but my supervising teacher was. Does your school offer professional development for that training?"

"That sounds so fascinating. That sounds a lot like another concept I learned about in undergrad. What can you tell me about that?"

4. **Attitude matters a lot.** Positivity, enthusiasm, energy, humor, and kindness will carry you a long way in your interview. This doesn't mean you have to be the human equivalent of a golden retriever puppy (some of the best teachers I know are unshakably calm and reserved) but, going back to one of my earlier points, think about what principals want to see in a candidate. They want someone they can envision communicating effectively with parents and interacting positively with students. They want a teacher who is motivated to know and love their students, not someone approaching their job with an "I'm just here to teach" dogma. They want someone who can get a group of children to do something they don't want to do, whether it's high school freshmen writing a literary analysis or first graders waiting in line for the water fountain without killing one another. (Equally difficult, by the way. I've done both. I substituted for first grade for two weeks one summer and am still recovering.)

5. **Don't focus solely on what a principal or interviewer says.** While the conversation in an interview is obviously important, remember that talk is cheap. To anticipate how your interviewer will act in the future, take cues from their actions as well as from what they said. Was the interviewer ready for you? How did they

treat their support staff? What was their body language like while talking about their faculty or school? Were there any hints of unprofessionalism or gossip? These observations will give you a better indication of what kind of work environment this person creates than a lot of what they might tell you directly.

6. **References matter way more than you think they might.** One of my former principals, a woman I like to call the LeBron James of education, always said that positive references and recommendations carry a lot of weight for a candidate in the interview process. So even if you don't have any teaching experience, you can make sure to include a lot of positive references from a wide variety of places—your supervising teacher, college professors, people who know you in the community, etc. If the online application asks for a minimum of two letters of recommendation but gives you the space to upload six and you have six people rooting for you, upload six.

7. **Have some questions ready for *them*.** In the part of the interview where the employer asks, "Well, do you have any questions for us?" it is really good to have a few questions ready to show that you're prepared and to demonstrate your expectations. These are the top questions a teaching candidate should ask their future employer, according to a Facebook poll of my readers, who are teaching goddesses and gods full of light and love and wisdom:

What kind of support is available for new teachers on your campus?

How is planning time structured at your school?

What will you miss about the person who held this position previously?

What has differentiated people who have been good in this role from ones who have been great? (The reader who suggested this pointed out that it's from *Ask a Manager* by Alison Green.)

What is the best thing about working here?

What supports are in place for the mental health of students at this school?

What kind of technology and supplies are available for teachers?

What is your favorite thing about the students on this campus?

What are the challenges and opportunities unique to this school?

8. **Try not to poop your pants, but even if you do, know that it still might be okay.** Once, as Love, Teach, I asked my readers for their worst interviewing stories for my own entertainment. A few hours after I'd posted my Facebook status, I got a message from a teacher telling me a story I will never forget: While waiting in the office for an interview at a school she was really excited about, she started to feel sick to her stomach. She desperately wanted to work at this school, so she willed her stomach to feel better. That worked for about thirty minutes. In the middle of the interview, she realized she did, in fact, *not* feel better. So she got up to excuse herself and at the same time *vomited all over the interview table and also pooped her pants.* I gasped probably five times reading her message, then laughed so hard I cried. So if you find yourself feeling like your interview was a disaster, just think to yourself: At least I didn't shit my pants. (She still got the job.)

As we discussed in the previous chapter, don't fall into the trap of thinking you need to find your perfect school on your first placement when you're interviewing. Again, this is definitely not true. I don't know anyone personally who found their perfect school immediately. I'm sure those teachers are out there, but most teachers I've talked to took several jobs at several different schools before finding a truly good fit.

And finally, don't believe that rejection means you are inadequate somehow or that it's necessarily because you royally screwed up in your interview. Nope. There are all kinds of reasons that the interviewer might have gone with another candidate, and sometimes the decision is unbelievably close. I got a whole new perspective on interviewing once when I was part of a panel interviewing new teachers for a position at my school. In the end, we were torn between two teacher candidates who were equally qualified and equally personable, and had equally stellar references. I forget how we ended up choosing (I think it came down to years of experience), but I remember thinking how much I wanted to call the rejected candidate and say, "It was SO CLOSE! We loved you! Do you want to hang out?" So if you lose out on a position and a principal tells you that it was a tough decision or that they hope you keep them in mind if another position opens up, just know that they likely mean it.

CHAPTER 3

Prepping Your Classroom

Allow me to tell you a story about the work I did setting up my classroom before my first year of teaching. Don't settle in—it's a short story.

I did nothing. At least none of the things I should have done. The end.

I remember a coworker of mine, a veteran teacher I'd met only a few days before, stopping by my room the day before school started.

"It's looking good in here!" she said, balancing a plastic tub on one hip.

"Thank you!" I felt a rush of excitement at having impressed a teacher who actually knew what she was doing.

"You staying late?" she asked.

"Oh, I think I'm pretty much done," I said.

My coworker looked around the room, nodding slowly. I know now what she was seeing—a room that made very little sense for teaching to take place. But at the time, *I'll figure it out as I go* was my mantra, which allowed me to go about my business, organizing pictures on my windowsill and filling my desk tray with flamingo-shaped paper clips, ignorant to the organizational hurricane inching closer and closer.

Fast-forward six weeks later and I still didn't have any classroom organizational plans. Walking around on a tour of my room, you would have found:

- A sort of modern art installation in one corner of the room made of giant white towers of varying heights made of stacks of paper.
- Uncapped markers and colored pencils in various stages of depreciation littering nearly all the flat surfaces of the room including the tops of file cabinets, bookshelves, and countertops.
- Small piles of paper throughout the room labeled with Post-it notes—some by class period, some with *No Name* or *Incomplete*, and one with the words *GRADE BY 08/21*. (It was nearly October.)
- A message on the corner of the dry-erase board that read: *Who left this mess?* with a sad face and an arrow pointing to the ground, identifying a Labrador-sized heap of crumpled construction paper and abandoned cardboard scraps.
- Students hunched over desks or standing, trapped among the class furniture and yelling at their classmates, "Ughh, *move!*" and "I can't! Where am I supposed to go?"[1]
- A campfire made with my most expensive school supplies burning in the middle of the classroom as my students gleefully roasted marshmallows over it. (Not really, but it felt close.)

---

1   The catchphrase "Where am I supposed to go?" essentially sums up my classroom and my experience teaching my first year.

I was struggling. I had little to no control over my classroom on many levels. And while a good part of the mess had to do with the fact that I hadn't yet grasped some larger, more complex areas of teaching like actual instruction and classroom management, I had no idea how much additional work and stress and confusion I could have saved myself by taking steps to make my room *work for me*. I didn't have places or procedures for students to access what they needed. I didn't have a seating arrangement that worked. I didn't have an organized way for students to turn in work or for me to return it.

Before I continue, just take a deep breath and understand that you will not encounter the same organizational hurricane that I did. You have not made your mantra *I'll figure it out as I go*—I know that because you're reading this book. Being aware of the importance of your space and taking steps to make it work for you might not make teaching easy, but it will make it easier. Anything you can do now to eliminate smaller frustrations and to save your energy for the bigger problems will be well worth it.

And remember this: The setup of your room can always, always be changed.

Setting up a classroom is tricky. Most teachers don't get to do it until they have their own classrooms for the first time. I don't know of any teacher education programs where student teachers help more experienced teachers organize their rooms in the summer, but even if they did, a lot of teachers might not have the wherewithal in the chaos of room organizing to stop and say why they're making the choices they're making, things like, "Hey, just so you know, I'm putting this pencil sharpener here instead of over there because I noticed it's better for student foot traffic" or "I'm spacing out the groups this far away so their backpacks don't get hooked on one another."

Setting up a classroom is also *expensive.* Teachers spend an average of five hundred dollars out of their own pockets on supplies and materials every year. And knowing what to pay for before the school year even starts can be especially daunting for a new teacher who, on top of having no experience and making a teacher's salary, is probably even more impaired by paying off student loans and barely having any savings. There's also the terrible and bizarre expectation for teachers to be martyrs, sacrificing everything from our personal time and our finances to our actual lives because we're supposed to be willing to do anything for our kids. I'll get to the issue of handling the expectations put on teachers more in chapter 14, but for now, know this: Being broke on behalf of your students will not make you a better teacher.

Here's the thing: Setting up a classroom isn't the most important thing in teaching, but it is *an* important thing. Setting up a classroom can make your teaching life a lot easier in a variety of amazing-yet-invisible ways. You may be focused on having a "perfect" room before the first day, but until you test out different supplies and layouts you can't know what you'll need to help your classroom run smoothly. Unfortunately, way too many teachers (including the one writing this book) go about it the wrong way when they are just starting out. As a result, you end up wasting personal time setting up an ineffective classroom—time that could have been used for curriculum planning or 1,295 more useful things. You waste money on unnecessary products, furniture, or decorations that don't add to classroom environment or functionality. In turn, having a poorly organized classroom wastes instructional time, since you can't do simple tasks like return work quickly or efficiently.

Wasted is not an adjective we want in a teacher's vocabulary.[2]

So . . . what's the right way to set up a classroom?

First of all, there's no "right" way. Each teacher is different, and each teacher has certain supplies, methods, and procedures they swear by. What works for one teacher might be tedious or pointless to another. To a certain extent, setting up a classroom is about figuring out what works for you, your students, and the way your classroom is run.

That said, there are some guidelines that apply to any classroom, whether you're teaching kindergartners or high school seniors. Though not exhaustive, here are several key areas that are important to consider and plan for:

SEATING

Seating is a crucial part of setting up a classroom that I virtually ignored my first year. It didn't seem like it mattered (or mattered that much), but I'm not kidding when I say it changed the whole feel of my room once I started paying attention to it. Having a seating arrangement that is actually functional is like putting half-and-half in your coffee instead of skim milk for the first time.[3]

Before you start making a seating arrangement, take a few minutes to visualize traffic patterns in your room. Picture a roomful of students walking in all at once, which is exactly what will happen multiple times a day. Is it easy for every student to get to their seat? To get up and sharpen a pencil before or during class? To make their way over to you with a question? Could *you* get to

---

2   During school hours, anyway.
3   For my vegan and noncaffeinated friends: like using coconut oil for making homemade popcorn instead of canola. LUXURY.

them in a room full of backpacks and humans? What about when you tell students to all get supplies from the same place? If you teach elementary: Will students trip over one another getting to the whole-group seating area on the floor? Trust me—I know the reality of giant class sizes in tiny rooms. It can be tough, but even just being aware of potential problems before they arise will save you and your students a lot of frustration.

Then, once you start teaching, adjust your seating arrangement as many times as you need. Don't be afraid to rearrange—even if it happens daily—until you find something that works for your students. Unless you're extremely lucky or you are some kind of unicorn, chances are you won't get it perfect on your first try. Don't know where to start? Peek in classroom windows around you to see how teachers with similar rooms and classes have their classrooms arranged,[4] go on Pinterest, or play around with scaled-down pieces of paper representing desks. It's also fun to ask students for their ideas on desk arrangements. One year, this led to my students and me having two long tables made up of desks we pushed together. It gave our classroom a "big family at Thanksgiving" vibe and freed up so much room for walking that we left it that way for the rest of the year.

When you find a seating arrangement that works, evaluate whether you can make it better. You may find you can free up space for yourself and for your students by getting rid of furniture, making trades with other teachers, or getting new seating through grants. Do you really need a giant teacher desk, or can you work with a smaller table? Do you need that small-group table, or can you have students bring clipboards to the

---

4   To clarify: Peek in if the classroom is empty. Knock on the door and introduce yourself if the classroom is occupied. Don't be the creepy new teacher.

floor? Could your students benefit from alternative seating options like couches or floor cushions? If you have excess furniture you don't want in your room, contact an assistant principal and they can arrange to have it removed and put in a collective storage area, or connect you with someone who will.

Just so you don't underestimate the importance of how much seating matters, I want to share with you a survey response I received in my third year of teaching. In the portion of the survey where I gave students space to tell me anything else I should know, one student wrote something like, "I want you to know that I really hate my seat. It's right up against the wall, and every day I have to ask the student next to me to scoot his chair so I can get through to my desk. I know it's annoying to him and I get so embarrassed, and sometimes I have to do this several times per class." I had no idea this was happening and was so, so glad this student said something. How hard would it be for me to work or concentrate or enjoy learning if every day I dreaded sitting in my actual desk?

Pro tip: Once you do find a seating arrangement that works, mark the corners of where the desks/tables should be with pieces of masking or painter's tape on the floor. This helps combat Desk Creep, a strange phenomenon in the teaching world in which desks migrate, unnoticed, up to several feet throughout the course of the day.

....

What You'll Actually Want in Your Teacher Desk

There are a lot of cutesy, picture-perfect back-to-school kits for teachers on Pinterest full of things like candy, mints, erasers, four Band-Aids. No, no, no. Here's what you actually need:

- A complete change of clothes, including shoes. Between exploding ketchup packets, giant rain puddles in the parking lot, student vomit, and surprise parent conferences on the day you've dressed up as a T. rex for Spirit Week, you'll eventually be very glad you have this.

- Kind of an entire pharmacy. You definitely should have ibuprofen or some kind of pain reliever, antacids, and cough drops on hand. But also think about having allergy relief, sinus meds, and other first aid you might need. (Check with your school's policy on having these drugs with you, and definitely keep these locked up.)

- Caffeine, if you're into it. Instant coffee packets, cans of espresso, nonalcoholic energy shots, or whatever you might need for a particularly bad 2:00 p.m. crash.

- Deodorant, toothbrush, and mouthwash. These have saved my life more times than I can count.

- Feminine hygiene products, if you have a period or teach people who have them.

- Thank-you cards, birthday cards, and envelopes. So handy around holidays, coworkers' birthdays, and Teacher Appreciation Week.

- A package of balloons and streamers for on-the-spot celebrations. In teaching, you *have* to celebrate the victories.

- Some filling snack, in bulk, that you won't be tempted to eat all of in one sitting. For me: protein bars or dried fruit. Everything else I can and will demolish in hours.

- Safety pins for wardrobe malfunctions. Once, a zipper that went halfway down the back of my skirt split wide open. I've never not had safety pins in my desk since.

Student Supplies and Organizational Tools

What exactly you'll need depends on a ton of variables: the age of your students, your content area, your teaching style, your students' learning styles, classroom size, how much funding your school has, etc. But no matter what or where you teach, before you buy ANY supplies from a store or ask students to bring them,[5] know your options to get things cheaper or for free. The money you will spend on your classroom will sneak up on you, especially at the beginning. A forty-dollar Target run doesn't seem too bad . . . until you make seventeen of them.

Before I continue, let me just make clear my thoughts on school supplies:

Teachers should not have to buy them.

Teachers should not have to ask parents to buy them.

Teachers should not have to ask other people to buy them via online fund-raisers, grants, social media pleas, or other methods of crowdfunding.

State leaders should make education an actual priority and provide our students the materials they need to learn.

But until that happens, here are my recommendations for acquiring supplies:

- Ask your school leadership. It never hurts to ask, and even if they say no, you will have communicated to your administration that you're invested in your students' education and getting them what they need. Many schools have a storage room with extra furniture, specific budgets

---

5   Be sensitive about asking for students and their families to provide supplies—most families love to help out in theory, but costs quickly stack up, especially at the beginning of the year.

dedicated only to classroom supplies, and supply closets you might not know about. Be conscious, though, if your school has to order the supplies you need, they could take a few months to come in depending on how large the order is and when it gets processed.

- Ask your coworkers. Teachers are the best kind of hoarders— the sharing kind. Sure, every once in a while you'll come across a dud who won't let you borrow one of five rolls of packing tape they have,[6] but for the most part, teachers know we're on the same side in this constant battle to get what we need to teach well. Just be kind and considerate and equally generous with your own stuff once you acquire it.

- Petition your social media following or e-mail contacts. Beg nicely with something along these lines: "Hey there, friends! I'm going to start teaching soon. Anyone have supplies they'd be willing to donate or know a retiring teacher I can connect with? I'm specifically looking for [whatever], but anything you can spare would be helpful. I can pick them up from you!" You may be surprised at how eager people are to do something that has a direct impact on education, or at least share your info with others who can help. I got a ton of my classroom supplies this way, and many people who didn't have spare supplies lying around wanted to buy me gift cards to office supply stores. I didn't stop them.

- Look into grants for teachers online or ask your district if they offer grants. It takes a little elbow grease, but almost every teacher I know has applied for and gotten a grant in some

---

6   I have more than five rolls of packing tape, but you can borrow them.

capacity to fund larger classroom projects for things like libraries or technology. It's a formal process—filling out an application describing your needs, your students, your school, and how the resources will be used—followed by a committee determining whether to fund your project. There's a very popular teacher grant company for Title I schools I've used several times with mostly positive results, but I won't mention them by name because for my last project they made my students write thank-you notes for refurbished technology *that we never got*, so that company is dead to me. However, it's worth mentioning that I've never heard of anyone else having a negative experience with them. Just be sure to run any grants you apply for through your school's leadership—some districts have restrictions and/or protocol you have to follow for donated items.

• Check out garage sales, secondhand stores, and dollar stores for certain supplies that don't need to be new or high quality. One year when my classes were close to forty students each, I removed a third of the desks in my room and got a couple couches from a garage sale to replace them, which freed up a *lot* of space. Also, a lot of times if you just tell people, "I'm buying these couches so I can help children love learning," they'll just give them to you.

• Don't be tempted to have everything by the first day of school. I can't emphasize this enough. Unless you're going to be cutting, gluing, crayon-ing, marker-ing, glittering,[7] and using construction paper or poster board on the first day of school (which I would not recommend doing unless you love

---

7   I am really loving *glittering* as an active verb.

misery), just get what you need (more on this in the chart that follows). You also may discover a secret grade-level supply closet you didn't know about, a department chair who works at Target on weekends as her second job and gets a discount, or find other ways of supplementing.

If you're like me and want someone to tell you exactly what they would recommend you need and don't need, look at this giant chart!

What You Need Right Away, What You Should Acquire Gradually, and What You Should Write Grants For/Wait Until You Win the Lottery:

Bare-bones essentials (i.e., you have nothing, your school is giving you nothing, and you are starting to teach this Monday):

- Pencils. You want as many pencils as you can physically amass. Some teachers have distribution/collateral systems for pencils, which is fine, but I'm of the opinion that ANY time I spend in pencil negotiations is a waste of my time. When I taught in Title I schools, I would ask for pencils for my birthday and those would last me a full year. To me, providing pencils without monitoring their return is five hundred trillion times less stressful than discovering a student who hasn't started on their work forty-five minutes into class because "I don't have anything to write with." I am done talking about pencils now.

- A good pencil sharpener. Look up reviews on e-retailers to be sure you're not getting a loud one.

- A good stapler. Seriously, don't skimp. You'll regret it when you find yourself constantly fishing out bent staples or uttering expletives as you throw your cheap one in the trash around December.

- Good dry-erase markers. You need several packs. Go EXPO or go home. Pro tip: Store them cap side down to extend their precious little felt-tipped lives.

- Homework/classwork receptacle. You need some sort of contraption for students to turn in their work that is not your hands or the surface of a table. My recommendation is a wooden mail sorter because you can have each class (or for elementary, each student) use a different slot. These can be pricey, though, so until you can afford one or the supply fairy visits you, use stacking plastic trays or a cardboard mail sorter.

- Hanging file crates/hanging files. You want to have one file per student. This is a superfast way of returning graded work to students AND if you notice that a student is absent, you can put handouts in their folder for when they return and ask you, "Did y'all do anything yesterday?" and you can say, "Yes! I already put the notes in your file," instead of "Welcome back! We took the day off and charted our astrology for the next month, ate pretzels, and talked about how much we missed you. Yes, we did something yesterday, but my teacher brain can't remember what. Give me forty-five minutes to find the handout."

- A way for students to keep track of their learning. This varies from teacher to teacher, but may be composition books, binders, folders, or some other method (don't go out and buy an entire class set, but just know you may have to supplement for students who can't get them).

- Kleenex and hand sanitizer. Keep these on your desk so you can make sure students don't drink your hand sanitizer. I'm not kidding.

To acquire gradually or via mini-grants:

- A big class set of markers, colored pencils, glue, and scissors that aren't terrible. If you don't have scissors, the kids will always be asking to borrow your nice pair and will never return them. And put your name on every last pair of those scissors, my friend.

- Supply storage bin. I've seen teachers have one bin per table, one bin per class, or one bin per supply (one for markers, one for glue, etc.). Hold off on buying these for a few weeks until you can make an educated guess on what will work best for your classroom.

- Those big Rubbermaid tubs. I think I have five, and they're still not enough.

- Additional good pencil sharpeners, staplers, and three-hole punches. Having multiple stations throughout the room really cuts down on traffic jams.

- Big Ass Post-it Notes. BAPINs. These are huge adhesive pads of paper that are great for demonstrating what the class is learning or helpful for students to show their group work.

- A set of clipboards. These are for those Cirque du Soleil students who like to work on the floor, bending backward over a chair, or hanging upside down from the ceiling.

- A set of small whiteboards with thin dry-erase markers for student use. A set of accompanying whiteboard erasers are a good idea, too, or you can repurpose old shirts or towels by cutting them up.

- All kinds of tape. You want to have Scotch tape for student use, painter's tape for taping off your whiteboard into sections, packing tape for any number of reasons. Put your name on all of it, too, or it will no longer be your tape.

- Paper towels.

- Cleaning wipes.

- Good erasers. Get the kind that won't tear up paper. I have a kind called Magic Rub, which is a great product name to have in a middle school classroom. Really. They've never commented on it once.

Big grant/Rich-aunt items

- Comfy alternative seating. Couches, squishy chairs, cushions, durable bean bags—all of these can be great and free up lots of room.

- Rugs.

- Ambient lighting.*

- Good speakers.

- A vacuum. This is useful for when cleaning staff doesn't come (this is an area that's been cut from a lot of public schools' budgets recently). A dustpan and broom are good for the same reason, especially for elementary, science, art, or shop classes.

- Mini fridge, coffee maker, and microwave* for days when you have to work through your lunchtime. Or if you schedule periodic alone time because you have introverted tendencies like me.

- Technology. Most schools don't have 1:1 technology, and it is totally worth trying to get a grant for a class set of laptops or iPads. I would recommend asking for five or ten more than your largest class size since technology can get wonky and IT help isn't always immediately available.

*Check to see if these are against your local fire code BEFORE acquiring any of them.

Do not need (or be very careful about buying):

- A themed classroom. This can be fun for kids, but it's not required for students to love your class or you. I've seriously seen teachers agonize over this and/or spend hundreds of dollars on décor they don't actually want. If your heart's not in it (and especially if you can't afford it), a themed classroom is just not worth it. I think my classroom's theme right now is probably something like "Weird, Colorful, Messy Family Room." It cost me zero dollars and my students love it.

- Twinkle or strand lights of any kind. Sadly, they're most likely against fire code.

- Most things from a teacher supply store. I have strong feelings about how overpriced this stuff is. I would recommend looking around at a place like this and then figuring out where you can find those things at half the price.

- Prizes. Personally, I tend to shy away from externalized reward systems related to learning, but I definitely don't recommend spending your own money on rewards for kids. There are so many free ways of rewarding your students that don't involve you paying for things. Once, I brought blankets to school and let my fourth graders set up blanket forts with their desks at the end of a unit, and they loved it so much I nominated myself for the Nobel Peace Prize. (I'm still waiting to hear back.)

Walls/Boards/Bulletin Boards

This one's easy. Leave it mostly blank except for:

- A poster with class expectations. I like to develop this collaboratively with my classes, which I'll cover in chapter 5, but if you want to start out with some basic rules, go for it.

- If you have a whiteboard, use painter's tape to divide a large section into a weekly calendar. This, I've found, is super helpful in giving students a visual for project deadlines and due dates. It also cuts down on "What are we doing today?!" which you will have to repeat twenty to a thousand times if students enter your room one at a time.

- Maybe a few decorative, inspirational, or instructive posters or signs. Regarding inspiration, I would say that unless YOU feel inspired by the poster, chances are it won't inspire your kids, either. Don't put things in your classroom (and especially don't buy things) purely to take up space. The exception here is elementary, which might need a few more anchor charts—big posters you make as a visual reminder of what students have learned—with things like the words to the Pledge of Allegiance, info about telling time, counting money, and other things I can still barely do.

Why leave walls mostly blank at the beginning of the year? Well, first, according to a December 2018 study published in the *Journal of Experimental Child Psychology*, filling up your walls with a ton of colorful visuals can actually be distracting to kids. Aim for engaging but not distracting, keeping 20 to 50 percent of the wall space clear.

Second, leaving space on your walls gives students an opportunity to fill them *with* you. Anchor charts and educational posters mean very little unless you create them with your students. It's meaningful and fun for kids, no matter their age, to watch their classroom fill up over the course of the year with their work and things they've learned. (Although if you ask a seventh grader, "Take a look around. Isn't it meaningful and cool to see what you've learned this year?" know that they will probably respond by saying something like, "Stop talking to me." But really, they mean yes. Man, I love teenagers.)

I know what you may be thinking: *But I've heard that my classroom needs to be warm and inviting—how I can I achieve that if my walls are mostly blank?* Don't worry, my friend. I, too, have a colorful, décor-loving heart. Here are some ways for you to add color/personality AND leave space for the rest of the year without breaking the bank:

- Add bulletin board fabric and signs to your bulletin boards that say things like "Outstanding Effort" or "Scientists at Work," which show students that 1) you have high expectations for their work; and 2) you're going to be filling these up soon. Hot tip: You can also use some funky, bargain-bin fabric to cover the sides of tables like a bed skirt so you have extra covered space in your room to store supplies.
- Laminate inspiring pictures, photos, or quotes as decorations.
- Keep colorful magnets on your board or file cabinets.
- Create a simple decoration on your classroom door—you'll find many ideas online by searching "classroom door."
- Create a big mural welcoming students the first day using butcher paper (most schools have this in their copy room or in the art room) or just using dry-erase markers or chalk on whatever kind of board you have.

Seven Things to Make Sure You Know Before School Starts

These are great things to ask a mentor teacher if you have one, or just the teacher you share a wall with if you don't. Some of these may be addressed in back-to-school professional development.

- How to use the copier. Make sure you know where to reload paper, how to print front-to-back, and how to staple, if yours has that function.

- Who to contact for technology and maintenance repairs. Once, during tutorials, I watched slack-jawed as hundreds of termites flew out of a hole in the wall. Make sure you have a contact person if something similar happens to you and put that number by your phone, because emergencies will erase your brain.

- The layout of the school. Especially on the first day of school, students will be asking you if you know where room 220 or the band hall is—make sure you can tell them!

- The protocol for calling in for a sub. Every school and district has a different procedure for this, including who you'll need to contact from your campus. Many districts also have online systems for requesting a sub, but these can be very tricky to navigate when you're using them for the first time at 4:30 a.m. when you wake up with strep throat the second day of school.

- How to send a student to the nurse. Some schools use passes from a special notepad, others just ask that the teacher writes a note and sends it with the student. But regardless, make sure your pass has your name, your student's symptoms, and the exact time you sent them—nurses have to keep records of these things.

- The cell number of your mentor teacher, teaching partner, and/or teachers on your team. Many teachers don't check their school e-mail past a certain time in the evening, so these will come in handy if you find yourself with a critical, time-sensitive question.

- Your school's policy on sending or taking students to the restroom. Again, different at every school. Some require hall passes, logs with space for names and sign-in/out times, etc. Also know that "anyone can go whenever they want" doesn't always work with kids.

Something to keep in mind as you're setting up your room is this: Your room is the easiest thing to change when it comes to your teaching. Do try to anticipate your students' needs, but don't spend too much time, energy, or money worrying about having everything you want right away. You can always, always, always adjust. Get creative. Talk to other teachers. Look on Pinterest (but don't despair comparing yourself to Pinterest Teachers). If you remember nothing else: Don't buy twinkle lights. Your fire chief will hate you.

Part II

Finding Your Groove

CHAPTER 4

Finding Your People: Creating Relationships with Faculty and Staff

In many ways, returning to school to teach is a lot like attending school as a student. Drinking in the fantastic, buzzing energy that pulses through the hallways on the first day. Adjusting to a life punctuated by bells. Getting accustomed once again to that disinfectant/pasta smell of the cafeteria. Oh, and the daunting task of navigating a large and diverse peer group and making the right first impression or they will hate you forever. (At least, that's the way school always felt to me as a person with high-functioning anxiety.)

I remember feeling that social stress as I headed into my first day of professional development when I started teaching. I didn't know anyone besides the principal I had interviewed with. The first-day jitters hit me *hard*.

Where would I sit?

What would we do?

Would they have me stand up in front of the faculty and tell two truths and a lie?

What should my truth be?

"I have a full-fledged unibrow if I don't pluck it regularly"?

"This game would be a lot easier if I were drinking a mimosa right now"?

"I've watched a Netflix documentary on Russian prisons . . . more than once"?

It must not have been too traumatic, because I don't remember anything more about that first day or the icebreaker activities. The relationships I formed and the experiences I had with the other people in that room didn't happen that day—they would unfold over the course of what ended up being two of the most transformative years of my life.

Jordan, another first-year teacher, was in the professional development meeting that day. She taught science down the hall and was part of a teaching placement program. Two months into the school year, I went into her room in tears to ask how she was so good at teaching while I was drowning, and she laughed and held up a student-created safety poster that read: PROTECT YOUR EYES: WEAR GLOVES. Jordan and I regularly laughed so hard we cried and ate gallons of queso in each other's company. On our last day working together, after we'd both decided to leave that school, we sat on the floor of my classroom and wept, wondering what the future held and whether teaching had made us stronger or had weakened us to the point of collapse. To this day, though she's several states away, we still check in with each other.

Ms. Santiago, a third-year science teacher who taught another grade level, was also one of the teachers in that first meeting. She gave me the lowdown on how things worked at our school: who you contact when you forget to punch in your time card, how to get through to the curmudgeonly secretary, and how to fix the copier when it jams. She offered to show me lesson plans that might work for my subject. She showed me a storage closet I had no idea existed. It was a series of kind gestures I'm still grateful for.

And then there was Ms. Dubois, a veteran teacher whose mere presence across the hall from my class was a thing of wonder. I observed a class Ms. Dubois taught in the spring semester of my first year. In that room, I got my first-ever glimpse of the type of teaching magic I desperately wanted: a classroom that was efficient without being cold, on task without being robotic, with students who were engaged and as trusting as they were trustworthy. Ms. Dubois showed me that the type of teaching I dreamed of was possible, and inspired me to dig and grow and fight until I had it.

Of course, there were also people I met initially who did not make my life better or brighter. But for the most part, the people in that room were people who, for two years straight, were rooting for me. A reading specialist who watched my class while I needed to fall apart on a particularly difficult day. A librarian who let my kids check out books even when I forgot to reserve the library (which was often). An assistant principal who listened to my deep and serious struggles with teaching without judgment and let me binge-eat her pretzel nuggets out of a giant canister. Thinking about these people makes me weepy, even now.

I cannot wait for you to find your people. Your relationships with other teachers and staff will be among the most important, meaningful relationships you ever have because no matter how many stories your boyfriend or roommate or parent or spouse has heard about what it's like being a teacher, no matter how much or how honestly you divulge to a therapist, the only people who can truly empathize with what it's like to be a teacher at *your* school are other teachers at your school. If you haven't found teacher friends at your school yet, don't despair! The *Love, Teach* community online is waiting for you with open arms.

The thing to remember about teachers is this: In many ways, we're all each other has.

To some people, this kind of advice may seem unnecessary. After all, even the most quiet and introverted teachers still enjoy people, so aren't relationships in the teaching world just kind of second nature? I had thought this, too, especially because I'd had little to no problems navigating relationships in my pre-teaching life, even with people I disagreed with. But dealing with other adult personalities in a school setting is about far more than just being nice to everyone or making friends. If you think handling relationships will be a breeze, ask yourself if you're completely sure you would know how to handle the following difficult situations:

- A popular veteran coworker on your team won't listen to anyone else's ideas, including yours.
- A coworker, one you actually like, regularly posts memes and comments on social media that are offensive not just to you but are also upsetting to the families of the students they teach.
- Some of your students approach you during class to tell you that their social studies teacher flirts with the boys in her class and it makes your students uncomfortable.

- An older coworker starts a bizarre rumor at school that the
  reason you never run out of copy paper is that you force
  your students to provide it for you.[1]

All of these scenarios are ones that either I or other teachers
I know have dealt with, by the way. And I'll tell you, navigating
them was not as cut-and-dried as we thought it would be.

So, how do you do it? Walking into a school full of strangers,
how do you find your Jordan and your Ms. Dubois? How do you
foster healthy and professional relationships with people who
might not necessarily be "your" people? How do you protect
yourself and your reputation from drama, gossip, and other
negative behaviors that bring down both the culture of a school
and your own teaching experience? Like any office or company
with varied levels of power, every school has its politics—how do
you stay out of them?

Here's what I recommend:

1. Come in with your hands open.

> One of the most crucial things to get right from the very
> beginning of any new experience is to approach it ready
> to receive as much learning as you can. Yes, you have had
> hours upon hours of teacher training—you may even
> have your degree in education. Maybe you come from a
> family of teachers (what a great support system, by the
> way!). And absolutely you will have awesome new ideas to
> share, and we want to hear them! But no matter where
> you did your training or how long you student taught,

---

1   I'll tell you right now that the last one was about me, though, and it still cracks me up
    years later.

you are about to experience a gigantic learning curve. There's no substitute for hands-on experience. You will discover people and ideas you can't wait to emulate . . . and those you would never want to emulate. But when it comes to your fellow faculty and staff, adopt the posture of an enthusiastic learner who's joining the team, not a maverick ready to take command.

2. Put yourself out there, but *juuuust* enough.

Go to everything. Go to the socials, happy hours, back-to-school bashes, and additional planning meetings at coffee shops. This helps communicate that you're a team player and open to meeting people; plus, it'll give you a better sense of who you want to really connect with and learn from and who you might want to limit your time with. (Introverts, I know that big groups of strangers can you make you feel a little panicky, but it's likely your keen observation skills can help you find the other introverts in the room.) And if your school is woefully lacking in social opportunities, nobody's stopping you from creating them yourself! Invite me if your social event involves cheese boards, dogs, or wine.

Be friendly, but keep your cards close to the vest for a while. One of the best ways to keep yourself out of any drama is to keep any critical opinions to yourself in the beginning. If a coworker irritates you or you don't like a decision about the new schedule, hold off on venting about it for now. But should you always keep these kind of opinions to yourself? There are teaching experts who might advise that schools ought to be "negativity-free zones," whatever those are, but I think that's both an unreasonable and dangerous expectation. Not only will we burn out if we try to pretend our teaching lives are perfect, but we will miss opportunities for growth if we can't discuss and sort through our struggles. My advice is to wait, even if it takes a while, until you have a source you can trust to not only keep your discussion confidential, but who—and this is critical—you trust to give you honest, tough-love feedback and not simply side with you regardless of the situation. Some of the most important growth I've had as a teacher has come when some of my kind and wonderful teacher friends have told me I'm missing the mark or given me perspective. I had a particularly challenging student in my class one year we'll call Sophia, and after lamenting to my favorite coworker, Vera, one day at lunch, she closed the lid on her Nutella, looked at me kindly, smiled, and said, "Look. I totally get that you're struggling—Sophia has a big personality. And I know volleyball is a different beast from English class, but she's not like that on the court at all. Maybe it's a relationship thing. I bet if you come to her volleyball game it would make her day." Vera could have nodded and said, "Oh my gosh, I know—kids these days, right?" Instead, she communicated that she valued me *and* my student enough to not let our rough patch continue. Pick teacher friends who will do the same for you.

Use social media with caution. Social media can be great for professional collaboration, but I would be very careful about using personal accounts to connect with others in your early days of being a teacher. I know teachers who will immediately go on a friending spree at a new school with other teachers and parents, citing it as a powerful way to connect, and I don't doubt that it is. But even if you feel that you have nothing to hide (personally, my Instagram is about as risqué as a Puritan's), being on social media can open you up to some things you might wish *you* didn't know about others—their weekend activities, political rants, oversharing about their personal life. My official recommendation is to change your name on social media or make your privacy settings unsearchable. But if you do decide to eventually "friend" people from school, know that it's kind of a slippery slope to being expected to friend everyone. *Everyone.*

3. Be kind, especially to those who are easily overlooked.

"Be kind to everyone!" is my party line, but make sure you are especially, go-out-of-your-way kind to the front office, cleaning staff, support staff, teachers' aides, and student teachers. Not only is it just worth it to be kind to everyone, but these people in particular don't get enough credit for the hard work they do behind the scenes that makes the school run. Added bonus: They can make your job a lot easier if you go the extra mile to treat them like the rock stars they are. Because I had a great relationship with a clerk at a former school, without my asking she exchanged my key for one that would open an interior door between my classroom and a neighboring one, making it way easier for us to collaborate. This isn't some kind of secret that applies just to the people who often get overlooked in schools; everyone does their job better when they feel valued. Also, it's funny talking about the "overlooked" in a school when, in fact, public education as a whole is already overlooked, but I digress.

4. Make sure you are carrying your weight as a new teacher.

Always taking without ever giving back is a very quick way to ensure that you'll get on your coworkers' nerves. It's true that you will need to do a lot of "taking" during your rookie years—of lesson plans, assessment ideas, supplies, teaching advice, etc.—and your coworkers should be understanding of and hopefully gracious about that. But even if you're doing a lot of learning your first year, you can still give back by:

~ Showing gratitude. Make sure those who are helping you know how much their time and effort mean to you and have helped your progress. A student teacher once made me a card with a construction paper donut on it that read, "You donut know how much you mean to me!" because she knew I loved both puns and carbs, and, clearly, I've never forgotten her gesture.

~ Making your coworkers' jobs easier. If you're borrowing lesson plans and resources, there's plenty you can do to pull your weight until you have your own pedagogical clout. Be the first to volunteer for the grunt work that you can actually do. Make copies. Run errands. Be the one to rotate bulletin boards. Offer to cover recess or lunch duty if a coworker is in a bind. If you hear your coworker stressing about something, start thinking about what you can do to help. Don't wait to be asked; look for needs and jump in.

~ Being available. It will be very hard for you to give anything back if your MO as a new teacher is to not be at school a second longer than required by your contract hours. I'm definitely not encouraging you to overwork or exhaust yourself—and I'm definitely recognizing that there are days where you *should* leave the first second you can. We all have families and pets and commitments and special circumstances, but if your before- and after-school availability is extremely limited in your first year for some reason, make sure you're checking in with your team or partner during conference periods or lunch to see what needs you can fill.

~ Bringing treats. Offer to pick up coffee or lunch every once in a while. Even if you're in a spot where you can't afford to pay for everyone (who can?), it's a nice gesture to even coordinate a delivery for lunch from a local vendor and have others chip in. Just make sure to check your school's policy on outside food delivery and give the front office coordinator a heads-up.

5. Establish boundaries with toxic people.

It's important for you to decide before you step foot in your school that you will not lend an ear to harmful gossipers or people who have adopted negativity as a lifestyle. Don't give them any space for saying demeaning things about students or other teachers, or you will find yourself on the receiving end of a daily half-hour rant by someone who is under the impression you enjoy hearing it.

You can do this kindly, by the way. My favorite lines to use are ones that acknowledge the feelings of the other person (which may be valid) without necessarily agreeing with them, and then either redirect their complaints or help orient them toward solutions.

~ "I can tell that this is important to you, so it sounds like you should talk directly to (person) about it."

~ "What solutions do you see for this problem?"

~ "I totally understand your frustration, and I value you as a coworker. [Person they're talking about] is a coworker I value, too. Have you tried talking to her about it?"

~ "I noticed you were frustrated about this same issue last week, too. What have you tried since then?"

6. Know the difference between solution-oriented venting and straight-up complaining. In the same way that you don't want other people standing in your doorway complaining about the same things every day, don't be that person, either! Always structure your conversation so that you are moving away from dwelling on a situation and moving toward a solution somehow.

"I'm at a loss for what to do about Ryan's behavior. Can you share some strategies that have worked for you?"

"I'm wondering if I was critiqued accurately on a recent evaluation. Can you come observe me and tell me what you think about my classroom management?"

"Since you were at the meeting, I want to know if I'm being oversensitive about that comment X made to me. Can you give me some perspective?"

7. Be brave about having tough conversations.

If you do find yourself needing to a have a tough conversation, it can feel anywhere from hard to impossible, especially as a new teacher. Maybe your team lead shoots down all your ideas, or your teaching partner isn't pulling their weight (we've all been there). But it's way better to have that tough conversation than to let those feelings fester and grow into resentment.

Let me tell you about a time I bottled up my feelings about a coworker for a whole year. His attitude, tone, and language toward me often felt condescending, and I was always either too intimidated or too embarrassed in front of kids to say anything about it. On the last week of school, he snapped at me in the teacher parking lot about picking up a delivery for me, and I *exploded*. Well, kind of. I knew I couldn't yell in the teacher parking lot, so instead I (bizarrely) whispered everything I'd been bottling up for the entire school year. He was stunned. A half hour later in my classroom, he came to me tearfully and earnestly, and explained that because I had never once said anything about his behavior, he assumed our relationship was totally fine. Then I felt horrible, too! Bottom line: We could have avoided the entire parking lot confrontation and my year of frustration if I'd simply been honest with him earlier.

I highly recommend the book *Crucial Conversations: Tools for Talking When the Stakes Are High*. This book (and the training, if your district will send you) not only helps you understand your own and others' approach and behavior in arguments, but walks you through practical approaches and even recommends certain vocabulary for talks that feel impossible. My favorite nuggets of wisdom from this book:

~ Start with heart. Start any tough talk by thinking about what you really want as a result and framing that into your discussion. "I really love being on the seventh-grade team, and I'm hoping to talk to you today about something that could make my experience better."

~ Turn villains into humans. Reframe the narrative whenever possible. This is a quote I've shared with so many student teachers I've had: "When you find yourself labeling or otherwise vilifying others, stop and ask: Why would a reasonable, rational, and decent person do what this person is doing?" This will help you see the humanity in the person with whom you have the conflict, and makes it a lot easier to approach the conversation as a misunderstanding.

~ STATE your path. After starting with heart, use the STATE acronym as a format for a crucial conversation to take.

  • Share your facts. "Sometimes I notice that when I share ideas at our meetings, you interrupt or roll your eyes." Make sure they stay facts!

  • Tell your story, explaining what you're beginning to conclude. "This has started to make me feel like my ideas aren't valued."

  • Ask for others' stories, encouraging them to share their side. "Do you have a different perception?"

  • Talk tentatively—share how you're interpreting the facts, but with room for you to be wrong. "I don't think you're intending to make me feel this way, but I'm beginning to feel discouraged."

- Encourage testing by making it safe for others to express opposing views. "That's a fair point," or "I completely understand that."

~ Move to action. End a crucial conversation by considering four questions: Who is involved in this action? What responsibilities does each party have? When will the actions take place? How will you follow up? Sometimes in a tough conversation you can forget to agree on these "terms," making it easy for a similar situation to pop up in the future.

If after this conversation things still aren't going well, you may need to either have a follow-up conversation or move up the chain of command to talk to a department chair and/or administrator. Handling interpersonal conflict is a part of any workplace, but neither bullying nor discrimination should be tolerated in any district.

Finally, don't be discouraged if you don't find "your people" right away. I get a lot of e-mails from lonely teachers, and I've been there. At some schools, I found my people right out of the gate, perhaps because the Teaching Gods knew I would be a hot mess without them. On other campuses, it's taken me longer— sometimes because it simply took longer to feel comfortable in a certain school, and other times because my schedule, the team I was on, or even my location in the school kept me more isolated.

Take your time.

Wait for the right people.

And in the meantime, make your Snapchat private.

CHAPTER 5

Getting the First Days Right

True story: Weeks before the first day of my first year of teaching, I did a Google search to see if I could find a script for what middle school English teachers say on the first day of school. No joke. I wanted it all written out for me. I wouldn't necessarily memorize it word for word, I reasoned—I might get creative with a few ad-libs, throw in a joke here or there. But I definitely wanted someone to tell me exactly what to say, how to fill that time, where to stand, what to do.

Like a play.

Or a weird, semi-scripted reality show.

Even though I'm at the point now where I would never need a script for the first day of school, I can *completely* understand and empathize with why first-year me thought I needed one. The idea of that first day of school bewildered me. In my student teaching, I had eventually gotten comfortable covering a full class period. But not only was my last day of student teaching months ago, I realized, it was in a classroom with established routines and procedures, familiar activities, students I knew, and a supervising teacher approving all my lesson plans. Under those conditions, it was easy to fill forty-five minutes or ninety minutes or however long we had.

But what about when it was just me?

And with kids I'd never met before?

Without any established rules or procedures?

And without a traditional "lesson plan" format?

And no Mommy?

. . . I mean, supervising teacher?

You don't need a script on your first day, either. You can definitely write one out for yourself to practice wording or timing, but I would advise against trying to memorize it. Even if you had a teaching expert craft a customized script for you, it would likely just assure that your students spent the first day thinking that you sounded like a robot. (Kids are way more perceptive than we give them credit for.)

You don't need to have every second of your first day planned impeccably. You also don't need your students to leave thinking you're the most amazing teacher they've ever encountered. What you need to do on the first day of your first year can be narrowed down to four pillars:

1. Ensure students are safe, comfortable, and where they should be.
2. Communicate high expectations for behavior and academics.
3. Start building relationships.
4. Plan something high-interest and memorable that all students will be good at together.

That's it. You don't have to go over your syllabus the first day. You don't have to point menacingly down a list of rules you've come up with. You don't have to start your curriculum. My former principal would say the same thing every year to us about lesson-planning when we had fifth graders visit our middle school: "I don't care what you do lesson-wise, but make sure they go home excited to return to your class." I believe that the same applies to your class on your first day of school. If you follow the four above guidelines for the first day, students will go home believing that your class is safe, that you have things under control, and that learning with you won't be the worst thing in the world.

Okay, that's it! Good luck!

Just kidding. I love doing that. Let me go a little bit deeper into what each of the four pillars entails.

ENSURE STUDENTS ARE SAFE, COMFORTABLE, AND WHERE THEY SHOULD BE

This is easily the most important pillar of the four. If you do nothing else the first day of school—your plans tank, the schedule is changed at the last minute, the fire alarm goes off because of a bag of popcorn in the teacher's lounge and you're outside for an hour in more than one hundred degrees of Houston heat—and at the end of the day your students are safe and on the right bus or in the right car or walking home in the right direction, you're allowed to consider your first day a success. And I salute you. Go home and eat a frosted strawberry Pop-Tart or whatever form your self-care takes.

There are a few things you can do to help this area of your first day go as smoothly as possible:

Get familiar with the first-day schedule, but anticipate interruptions and changes. Your school will provide this schedule for you, however, I've been at several schools that won't give it out until a day or two before the first day, not because they delight in leaving teachers in the dark, but because there truly is an insane amount of work involved in making a master schedule. Master-schedulers are also often trying to do eighteen other things at the same time.

But when you do get that schedule, go over it ten times and walk through the whole thing in your mind. If there's any part of it you don't understand or need clarification on, don't e-mail someone about it—call or go see them in person to find out exactly what "take manual attendance" means, or where your bus duty location is. It's possible that your question might expose an actual problem with the schedule or provide an opportunity to clarify it for other new teachers. Knowing the schedule like the back of your hand might not make your first day perfect, but it will help things go much more smoothly than a figure-it-out-as-you-go approach where every five minutes you're checking your clipboard and/or the clock.

That being said, understand that first-day schedules in the teaching world are very . . . flexible. It's likely that you will have all kinds of unpredictables on the first day. Between children coming in late because of the enrollment process (or spending fifteen minutes in the wrong room by accident), administrators popping in to give you a heads-up on a schedule change, a seven-minutes-long announcement from the front office on the speakers, a parade of parents dropping off students and school supplies (I'm looking at you, primary teachers), and other people and events you didn't anticipate, it will be very beneficial for you to have a roll-with-it attitude. Remember: What matters most is safety and student comfort. That's your main goal.

On the first day, make it abundantly clear for students that they are in the right place. Make sure your classroom is labeled clearly with your name on the outside. No matter what age you teach, make sure your name is very clearly displayed on or outside your door. If you teach secondary, add your course name to your door tag outside (if it's not already there), write your name and course name inside your classroom on the board, and copy the day's schedule with times onto the board for teenagers who may have already lost theirs. If you teach elementary, have your students' names on display outside your classroom and inside as well on desks, cubbies, bulletin boards, etc.—it's also a good idea to save spaces, labels, and desks for students who might be enrolling late. The goal, no matter what age you teach, is for students to walk in and know, *This is where I'm supposed to be. I belong here. I'm in the right place.* This will also help prevent the highly embarrassing situation of a student sitting through half of your class before realizing they're in the wrong room. Poor wrong-room angels.

If you're an elementary teacher, make sure you know how each of your students is getting home at the end of the day, and check with your school on the procedures for bus lines, car riders, kids who walk home, etc. This is critical both for safety and students knowing they're in the right place.

Know that it's better to err in the direction of over- instead of under-structuring your classroom. Even though it's important to have a go-with-the-flow attitude when it comes to interruptions and surprises the first day of school, it's also important to communicate to your students that you have things under control. It is way, way, way easier to start off highly regimented and then gradually loosen things up than to start off loosey-goosey and try to implement structure later on. So, if you're not sure whether to assign seventh-grade students their seats or let them choose on the first day, go with assigned seating in the beginning. If you're not sure whether your second graders should walk to the library silently in a single-file line or talking quietly, choose the silent line. If you're not sure whether you should have high school sophomores sign in and out to use the restroom or just let them go, have them sign in and out. If you find yourself making any kind of choice between "Should we do this the regimented way or the less structured way?" on the first day of school, choose the former. You can always decide later if you want to relax your policies.

Understand that you may have some student meltdowns—and make sure you don't melt down in response. The first day is a high-stress time for everyone, including your students. Be responsive to but not alarmed by tears or panic—this is very normal for the first day or even weeks. Between the anxiety of a new schedule, the adjustment to a new bedtime/wake-up time, and social interactions, student meltdowns are bound to happen. Respond in a way that shows you care about their feelings, but that they haven't done anything out of the ordinary.

Even if you're not sure how to respond, you can make it seem like you know what you're doing. For example, let's say the fire alarm goes off the first day and you've completely forgotten which evacuation route your class is supposed to take. Staying calm and peeking into the hallway to see what nearby teachers are doing before taking action will probably make your students feel more secure than if you started pacing and saying, "This is probably not a drill. Would any of you like to be in charge?"

COMMUNICATE HIGH EXPECTATIONS FOR BEHAVIOR AND ACADEMICS

Despite what a lot of teaching books and experts might tell you, I (and a lot of other teachers out there) don't think you need to go over every single one of your rules and syllabus in-depth on the first day of school. The thinking there is that kids need to know rules and expectations from the get-go for there to be order (and if you'd feel more comfortable doing this on your first day, by all means, do it), but there's no reason you can't go over rules the second day of school or in small chunks over the course of several days. Even for districts that mandate that all teachers in a certain subject teach the same things on the same days on a calendar (I have a huge problem with this, by the way), you can catch up if you take a different approach to the first day. I promise.

But even if you're not using the first day to give the lay of the land, there's a lot you can do to communicate that you have things under control and that students need to have themselves under control when they're with you.

Teach at least one procedure on the first day. I say "at least" because most elementary teachers will have their students all day and can start students on several procedures, but secondary teachers have time for at least one.

On the first day of school, I start teaching students how I get their attention. There are a thousand great, creative ways of getting students' attention, but I do a simple countdown (with several seconds of pausing in between each number): 5 . . . 4 . . . 3 . . . 2 . . . 1. I tell students what the procedure is and explain to them why I do it the way I do; the countdown gives them time to finish their conversations—and I respect their conversations—but that all talking and noises should be wrapped up before "1." I tell my students we're going to practice several times over the next few days. "But don't worry—if you're having trouble still talking after '1,' I can give you more opportunities to practice— we'll figure out a time convenient for you." Then I say, "Okay, let's practice! Turn to your neighbor or get a group of three and talk about whether you'd have a lobster claw or an octopus tentacle for an arm. Go." I wait awhile for their conversations to ramp up, then I count down. There is always, ALWAYS at least one kid grinning at me goofily who keeps talking past 1, and I say, smiling, "I had a couple of voices still talking when I got to 1, but that's totally fine. We'll keep practicing until we can all get it right."

Teaching at least one procedure from the first day of school is almost less about the procedure itself than it is about showing students you respect them and their time and that you are in charge of a safe and respectful classroom. I just choose this one because it's one of the procedures I find myself needing the most in chatty middle school classrooms, and because I will die of old age if I do the wait-it-out method of getting students' attention—that is, a teacher saying, "I'll wait," and then staring at kids until they get quiet. It's a strategy I saw listed in multiple teaching books, and in my experience works with about five students in maybe 2 percent of classrooms. More on procedures—especially for younger kids—later in this chapter.

Redirect any students who are off task or not doing things the way you ask. As a brand-new teacher, I had this fear of correcting my students when they weren't doing what I wanted because I thought I'd be perceived as mean. I invite you to imagine what my classes were like under this philosophy. I'll wait until you're done laughing.

Relationships are critical from day one, but so is setting yourself up as an adult who has things under control. Be clear, firm, polite—and make sure your face is communicating those things instead of anger or sarcasm. Give them the benefit of the doubt, whether you're speaking to the whole class ("I know we're getting close to the end of the day and you're exhausted, but right now I need to see all eyes on me and all heads upright. Thanks!") or an individual ("You may have forgotten, so I'll remind you: My instructions at the door were to come in quietly and get to work on the survey on your desk. Can I see you doing that, please? Thanks so much.").

If a student still won't comply, continue being firm but kind and, in private with the student, say some version of, "I can see you're having trouble staying on task. I would love for us to talk about how we can work together to make it easier to do that. I'm happy to give you opportunities to practice staying on task. Do you want to go ahead and give it one more try, or should we plan on setting aside a couple of minutes in the next few days to practice?" Just make sure you're not delivering this as a sarcastic threat—you'll lose them if there's any hostility in your tone. Some students may go as far as to take you up on this, but the combination of not having an audience and wishing they were doing anything else will have them demonstrating the procedure pretty quickly.

Plan way more for the first day than you will be able to get done. Show students from the first day that they will be expected to utilize as much class time as possible. This isn't to say you should teach up until the bell and not give students time to get packed up, but you don't want to find yourself with twenty spare minutes at the end of class for you to spend shrugging your shoulders and announcing, "Well, I guess you can have free time?" I try to have students working until one or two minutes before the bell, but if I find myself with a few minutes to spare on the first few days of school, I use that time to practice names and invite students to play a game and challenge the time it takes me to name everyone in the class. They always lose.

START BUILDING RELATIONSHIPS

Don't be intimidated by this step—you shouldn't have students tell you their life stories, talking about their greatest fears, or really doing anything more vulnerable than the already-vulnerable act of participating in the first day of school. However, there are baby steps you can take, even on the first day of school, to show students you are invested in their growth and in them as people.

Greet students at the door. Do this for sure on the first day, but also do it every day (more on this in the next chapter). I'll be the first to tell you how hard it is as a new teacher to greet students at the door when you're also expected to check your e-mail, prepare for the next class, and do a hundred other things we have to do every day in addition to teaching. But greeting students isn't just a research-proven way to positively affect student engagement and the speed at which they get on task; it's a kind gesture that says, *You are worth me getting up out of my chair.* Safety bonus: It helps you keep an eye on any hallway insanity.

Start learning their names, including correct pronunciations. I may not ever remember where my keys are or what my password for my insurance provider is, but I have my student names memorized by the end of the second day of school. Even when I had thirty-five students per class, even when a good chunk of my students' names were ones I was unfamiliar with, I made it a priority and learned them through lots of repetition at home.

Pronounce your students' names correctly, even if you have to write it down phonetically and practice it. Some students may ask you to use a nickname, and that's fine, but don't automatically default to a pronunciation that's easier for you—it's insulting and, quite frankly, lazy. If someone met me and said, "Kelly?

Yeah, I'm not going to do that. Is 'Carly' okay?" I would frown and ask, "Can I un-meet you?"

It's a good idea if your students are old enough to write to have them make desk tags, pieces of paper folded into triangular prisms with their names on the face that is visible when they're sitting upright. Be sure you have them print in large letters and with dark marker, and either collect the desk tags at the end of class or have them put them somewhere other than their pocket so you can keep learning their names during the next few days. Also there are a thousand cuter ideas than paper prisms on Pinterest; just search "desk tags for students." I just like the prisms because they're the easiest for me to see.

Take time to let students know who you are. Sometime in the first few days of school, I show my students a five-minute Google Slides presentation that includes a particularly awesome picture of my bangs/braces situation in middle school, an overview of my family and interests, and descriptions of what past students have said about me as a teacher and about my class—the good, the bad, and the laughable. I tell students that if I expect to get to know them, I feel like they should have an opportunity to know me and who I am. Be careful that this isn't a "look at how perfect my life is/how cool I am" presentation, though—that might feel eye-rolly and unrelatable.

PLAN SOMETHING HIGH-INTEREST AND MEMORABLE THAT ALL STUDENTS WILL BE GOOD AT TOGETHER

Whether you have elementary students for the whole day or secondary students on a shortened schedule, you can eliminate a ton of student anxiety by having at least one game, activity, or low-key "lesson," especially since on most secondary campuses, classes are shortened the first day. It's very important that you make this an activity that a wide range of abilities can experience success with—consider that there's a good chance you may have students who are struggling with English, have a learning challenge of some kind, or have been conditioned to hate school because they feel unsuccessful. Plan things that will have all your students walking away feeling good (or at least not feeling panic attack-y) about your class this year.

Every school is different, but here's an idea of what three different teachers plan for the first day of school.

What My First Day of School Looks Like: Elementary

Teacher: Catherine Perez

Grade: 1st

School: Title I elementary, Houston, TX

Class period: All. Dang. Day. (6 hours)

1. I have a coloring activity or other simple worksheet on each desk with community pencils and crayons in the middle of each table for when students enter and parents are moving around. Think simple and chose an activity that requires no teacher support since you will be greeting students and parents and helping everyone find their place. (Note: making and decorating a name tag would work with older elementary students.)

2. I conduct a whole-group "meeting" to teach the procedure for how I get the students' attention and how to come to the whole-group area (if the class is a primary grade). I also teach how I want students to enter the room and where to put things, and then we *practice*. We actually put our backpacks back on and grab lunch boxes then head to the hallway to pretend we are coming in the room for the first time.

3. Back to whole-group meeting. During this time:

I go through names. I ask students to introduce themselves to the group—this can be a game, a "say your name and your favorite color" thing, whatever—but we repeat each student's name back to them so that we can all practice pronunciation. I remind students that we are a "family" and that learning each other's names and the correct pronunciations is extremely important—how silly would it be if you didn't know your brother's or sister's name?

I check to make sure I know how each child is getting home that first day. Some teachers ask this at the meet-the-teacher event (which I recommend) but also ask parents as they drop off their children—make phone calls or call the front office to have them call parents if you aren't sure.

4. We do a school tour for new students and as a refresher for returning students. First, we practice how to line up, then we hit the major spots: bathrooms, office, ancillary/specials classes like PE and art, cafeteria, attendance clerk, etc. It's very important to show students the dismissal locations!

Plan more time than you think you need for the tour for students to practice the procedure of how you want them walking in the hallway. Keep stopping if needed and reminding students of the procedure until you have 100 percent compliance from every student.

5. My extra plans depend on how much time is left in the school day. We sometimes read a book or two aloud, do a brief writing assignment (on topics like "about me" or "what I liked best about summer"), and/or sort supplies and materials if students brought them ("Put all of your pencils in this box. Put crayons in your pencil pouch," etc.). It's a good idea to have several other name games or community building activities ready.

6. Dismissal!

What My First Day of School Looks Like: Middle School

Teacher: Me!

Grade: 6th–8th English

School: Non Title–I middle school, Houston, TX (though I used this format for Title I schools as well)

Class period: 50 minutes

1. I greet students at the door holding a coffee can with popsicle sticks in it, each labeled with a number. I have each student pick a popsicle stick and then find the desk inside with their corresponding number. I say very clearly, one at a time, "Hi! What's your name? I'm so glad you're here! I'd like you to go inside, find your desk, and then get started with the task on the board." (The directions on the board walk them through how to make a name tag for their desk so I can start learning their names—I also provide pictures for each step.)

2. When the bell rings, I come inside and say how excited I am to see students following directions, but I also add (with no sarcasm!), "Don't worry—if you forgot the directions at the door, I'll give you tons of opportunities to practice this week for you to get it right" (1 minute).

3. I give a very brief introduction telling my kids I'm so excited they're here, they're in good hands, and we're going to learn a lot this year. I also explain that while I do have a syllabus and expectations, we will create the expectations together and go over the syllabus tomorrow. In the meantime they can find my syllabus online if they're curious tonight (2 minutes).

4. Then I introduce and practice a procedure in preparation for a whole-class activity (i.e., "I'm going to show you how I plan to get your attention this year, and we'll practice it in the activity we're about to do) (5 minutes).

5. I run a whole-class activity that ties into why my class matters—not because "you need to know this in high school" or "it'll help you in college" or "it'll help you get a job," but because stories are who we are and how we connect with other people, because our voices matter and being able to communicate that voice clearly matters, etc. In the past we've done group murals, watched Chimamanda Ngozi Adichie's TED talk on the danger of a single story, sorted ourselves into six categories based on which piece of art I've projected on the board we identify with most and then discussed it—I change it up each year.

6. I wrap up with some kind of journaling, survey, or independent creative activity that I know will keep them working until the bell and that we can pick up the next day (however long until the bell rings).

What My First Day of School Looks Like: High School

Teacher: Colleen Carey
School: Fremont High School, Sunnyvale, CA
Course: College Prep Chemistry
Class period: 45 minutes

1. On one of my prep days before school, I write all my students' names on notecards and put them in stacks by class period. This makes it easy to put them on desks and get kids to their seats for my first seating chart.

2. Before the bell rings, I put the notecards with names on desks, and I start playing some very happy/good mood music really loud. I greet students at the door and tell them to follow the directions on the slide I've projected onto the board (about 3 minutes).

WELCOME TO COLLEGE PREP CHEMISTRY!

1. Find the seat with your notecard on it and sit in that seat.

2. Introduce yourself to the people at your table.

3. Find at least two things that every person at your table has in common.

---

3. I introduce my attention grabber. I have a three-note chime that for some reason isn't tuned properly and the top note sounds horrible—everyone hates the top note! So when I'm ready to move on, I play all three notes of the chime slowly and see if they stop talking. Then, I vow to never play the top note if they are quiet by the second note. This works really well for getting attention, and I find that my high school students respond well to it as it's not a "childish" attention grabber, but also there's something in it for them if they're quiet fast enough. We practice a few times (2–3 minutes).

4. I welcome them! I tell them my name, and have them answer some questions on their notecard (slide provided below). We practice turning things in and picking up handouts. Now I have notecards with their names on them that I can shuffle and use for future seating charts and to help learn their names (5 minutes).

NOTECARDS

On the front:

- If you go by a different name than what is on the card, please write it below your name so I can learn it. Please also include your preferred pronoun.

- Below your name, write any seating preferences you might have (ex: "Near the front."). If you don't have a preference, write, "No preference."

On the back:

- Tell me (or draw!) something about yourself.

---

5. Introduce the rock activity. I have students talk for a minute or so at their table group about the difference between qualitative and quantitative observations. When they have had a chance to talk to their group, I get their attention (using my three-note chime) and ask for volunteers to give me a characteristic of qualitative or quantitative observation. Once they nail it (or if I have to fill in the gaps), I'll display the slide on the next page and review the differences, asking students to record this on their worksheet (5 minutes).

Observing Rocks

Qualitative Observations	Quantitative Observations
Describes qualities of a thing	**Describes a thing using numbers (quantities)**
Color, texture, smell, sound, taste, feel	Height, weight, number of stripes, distance
Make as many observations of your rock as you can. Make at least *10* qualitative AND *10* quantitative.	

6. With the slide still showing, I give each table a rock (one of those small white rocks for between pavers that you can get at a home improvement store). While students are making observations about their rocks, I go through my notecards to see if there are any names that are different than what is on my seating chart, then I go around to each group to introduce myself to each student and make sure I have the correct pronunciation of their name. I also ask them what their group has in common (the question on the board from way back at the beginning of class) and check in on their observations. I give them about

15 minutes, or however much time so that I have 15 minutes remaining with the rest of class.

7. Once I decide it's time to move on, I have one representative from each group bring their group's rock to one table (you can spread this out between several tables, too). Then, I mix the rocks around and tell students to work together to find their group's rock based on their observations. At first it seems impossible, but eventually they'll find them (about 5 minutes of pure chaos).

8. I get students' attention again using the three-note chime and ask them to head back to their assigned seats and answer the questions on the board (see below) on their worksheet, working silently. For the few remaining minutes in class, we discuss our answers (about 10 minutes total).

OBSERVING ROCKS

1. What did you realize about your first observation?

2. If we did this activity again, name some specific observations you would add when you first get your rock.

3. How can you apply what you've learned from today's lesson to the "bigger picture" outside of science class?

Even though these lesson plans are different from each other in both the age they're geared toward and in content, I want to point out how each of them—even during the chaos of the first day of class—honor the students in the class in ways that may seem small, but start laying the foundation for great relationships.

Each of these lessons has the teacher communicating and modeling the importance of knowing how their students' names are pronounced. None of the lessons require students to have prior knowledge to participate or feel successful or demand that students talk about their family or home lives or other (unfortunately) popular topics that are likely to be sensitive for so many students.

On your first day, remember that what matters is not that everything goes the way you envisioned it in your head. It's okay if your students had more trouble following directions than you anticipated, or if students only got five minutes into the activity you planned before it was time to pack up. It's okay if you forgot to hand out your parent letter to one class to read over at home or if one class was ten minutes late to lunch because you misinterpreted the schedule even though you read over it thirty times. If your students left your class safe, with all their body parts intact, and believing that your classroom is a safe place for them, then you had a good first day.

First-Day Survey Questions Students of All Ages Will Actually Want to Answer

You know those back-to-school "About Me" questionnaire sheets that a lot of teachers ask kids to fill out the first day of school with their name, favorite color, favorite subject, etc.? While those are great, I've found I get to know my students a lot better by asking them short-answer questions that reveal their personality, thought process, and sense of humor. Feel free to use these questions that my readers and I came up with for a survey, topics for a persuasive paper, or a class discussion when you can tell kids need a brain break:

Would you rather have to dance every time you moved, or sing everything you spoke?

Would you rather get a one-time check for $15,000 or get paid $10 every time you sneeze for the rest of your life?

You've been appointed to rename the giraffe. What do you name it?

Describe two ways life would be like if you weren't able to tell the difference between a shoe and a sandwich.

What problem in the world do you most want to solve?

Would you rather be a giant (skyscraper-tall) hamster or a tiny (thumbnail-sized) rhino?

Would you rather have a cat with a human face or a dog with human hands?

Would you rather be the best player on a team that always loses or the worst player on a team that always wins?

What's your favorite song right now? (Note: The teacher who suggested this compiles her students' favorite songs into a playlist and listens to it on the way to/from the first weeks of school!)

The answer is 9 penguins. What is the question?

....

CREATING A SUCCESSFUL CLASSROOM IN THE FIRST WEEKS

The first day is important for first impressions, but you will need to keep up the energy and momentum over the coming weeks as you begin to build a class culture, fine-tune classroom management, and build relationships with your students. Here are some things to keep in mind as the first few weeks unfold.

The First 1–2 Weeks of School Should Be Procedures Boot Camp

I talked about a first-day procedure in the first half of this chapter. I can hear your questions. But how do the rest of them work? What are procedures? How can anyone teach rules/policies/procedures for one to two weeks when curriculum is supposed to start almost immediately? Aren't rules and procedures for little things kind of insulting, especially for older kids?

First of all, read the section about procedures in *The First Days of School* by Harry Wong. He explains all of this way more in-depth than I can. But basically, the idea is that procedures show your students the way things work—clearly and in-depth—so things go smoothly and you and your students can focus more on what matters for the rest of the year. "Going over procedures" isn't simply reading off a list of your rules and expecting students to remember them; it's an entire process. You start by introducing the procedure, having students practice it until they can't get it wrong, and then returning to practice if the procedure gets "forgotten." It may feel silly, but would you rather feel silly for a few minutes at the beginning of the year having students practicing lining up, or feel like a crazy person asking students to line up quietly a thousand times and having no one listen to you from September until May?

I don't use all the recommendations in Wong's book, but every year I teach my students and have them practice all the things that drive me nuts or that I find myself repeating over and over unnecessarily, things like:

- Entering the classroom: The procedure is to walk in quietly, read the board, get materials, be seated, and follow directions.

- Getting students' attention: My students should listen for the 5-4-3-2-1 countdown and be silent with their eyes on me before 1 (anyone still talking after 1 will need to practice).

- Using the supply closet: Students should take only what they need, close the closet door so Ms. Treleaven doesn't break her wrist on the steel handle, and return materials when done.

- Using the pencil sharpener: I tell them to use it literally any time other than when I'm talking to the class.

- What to do during various drills, lockdowns, etc: I didn't think I'd need to tell students to be silent during emergency drills. I was wrong.

For younger kids, procedures are even more important to practice because they can take a little longer to master. Here's what the elementary teachers I know go over with their students:

- ☐ How to come into the classroom and where to put things

- ☐ How they will get students' attention

- ☐ How to line up and move through the hallway

- ☐ How to get ready, clean up, and pack up at the end of the day

- ☐ How going to the bathroom works (Will they go as a whole group or on an individual basis? Will they raise their hand and ask out loud, or have a silent hand signal? Etc.)

☐ Expectations for workstations/group work/
transitioning to new activities

☐ Expectations for library, cafeteria, recess, and other
regular activities

☐ What emergency drills are and what students are
expected to do during them—talk to your school or a
veteran teacher on your team about how/when is best
to do this

If you're understandably panicking about the idea of teaching procedures for one to two weeks considering the teaching you have to do, don't worry—I'm not suggesting you have students line up and sit back down for entire class periods. You can teach these procedures through the instruction you've already planned. Teach the procedure for lining up on the day you have a library trip or are heading to the biology lab. Teach the procedure for when they can sharpen pencils on the day they take one of five thousand mandated diagnostic tests at the beginning of the year. Practice the procedure for getting students' attention on the first day you assign group work.

Have Students Help You Create Your Class Rules/Expectations

I've found that when I've given students a say in making our classroom rules or norms, they are way more likely to follow them. Sometimes, usually on the second day of school, I ask my students for their help in coming up with norms or guidelines so we can have the best year possible. If there's a certain area I feel like we've skipped over, I'll direct them toward a discussion about it. For example, my school allows students to have snacks, but I really don't like for students to bring snacks that end up leaving messes either from crumbs or greasy fingerprints. So in our rule-setting, if we haven't created a norm for snacks, I'll say something like, "What do you think about snacks? Can you think of any reasons we should have boundaries? What kinds of snacks might create problems? What happens if my last-period class leaves a mess and I don't catch it—whose job have we made harder?" That way, students come to the conclusion themselves about which snacks to avoid bringing. Usually we end up with about twenty norms and I ask them for help in simplifying them into "umbrella" rules, things like *Make choices that respect others and yourself.* Limiting snacks to non-messy options falls under this rule, but so do other situations that are hard to anticipate, like when a student decides to use an entire row of unused staples, a ruler, and half a roll of Scotch tape to make a back scratcher for himself.

One thing I always address during this time is that my classroom is a safe space for all students. It's critical for each of my students to know right away that I won't support or allow any behavior or speech that demeans the personhood of another group. More on how I word this in chapter 6.

Although elementary-age teachers think they may have to spell out every rule for their younger students, you'd be surprised how close they can get to a solid set of rules if you allow them to brainstorm. You'll likely have to steer them in the direction of a few rules they'll miss, but the payback is letting them feel that they have agency in the classroom. And, yeah, first graders might say they've decided on a class rule that every day has to begin with a dance party, but you can do one of two things: 1) segue into how great it is that they've touched on a rule about enthusiasm and participation, 2) adopt a new dance-party class rule, because really, how fun would that be?

I've also found that when my students and I come up with

expectations together, they're more likely to take ownership of their actions and accept consequences. It's harder to disagree with a rule that you had a role in creating.

Don't Be Afraid of Feeling Like You Have *No Idea What to Do*

Sometime during the first week I was teaching, one of my first period eighth-grade students opened the door fifteen minutes after my class had started, shouted, "BYE!" to his friend in the hallway, and then continued eating a pint of ice cream he was holding.[1] It was too difficult for my brain to even process the number of offenses at that point—lateness, disruption, ice cream—and I had no idea what to do. Let him finish his ice cream? Confiscate it and eat it myself? Leave my class unsupervised for five minutes while I put it in the faculty freezer *for him?* I'm not sure how long I stared at him, frowning, slack-jawed, watching him pick out large pieces of chocolate cookies with his spoon, but it was definitely long enough for my class to start laughing nervously and for my face to turn magenta.

New teachers get understandably stressed about the first days of school—the activities, what they'll say, how their kids will respond. But I think instead of preparing with the goal of eliminating any and all uncertainty, new teachers should *prepare for uncertainty*. They should prepare to have no idea what to do. They should prepare for a couple of moments of panic. Not in a panic-inducing, scary movie, screeching violins type of way in which something terrible and unknown is lurking around the corner, but in the way you feel opening a pressurized can of biscuits,[2] knowing that the loud *pop* is inevitable, and laughing

---

1 This was not in a snack-friendly school.
2 Surely I'm not the only one who has this reaction to biscuit cans.

at yourself after it happens and how you jumped a foot in the air and scared your dog.

I know it's uncomfortable to think about having no idea what to do. We like to be in control, to feel as if we are completely prepared. But there is so much value in the "I have no idea how to handle this" struggle. Every time you awkwardly flop your way through a tricky situation, you are learning how to get yourself out of something similar in the future. You're adding to your toolbox, your portfolio, your "Oh, shit" file cabinet.

If you're wondering what I did about the ice cream situation I mentioned earlier, I'm 90 percent sure I went across the hall and asked a more experienced teacher what I should do. But there's no question I would know how to handle it better now. I would take exactly eleven seconds in the hall to tell the student privately, "Hey, I love ice cream, too! You reminded me that I haven't talked about my no-ice-cream-in-class policy since it can get messy. So go ahead and eat it today, but in the future, ice cream stays outside. Deal?" This way I:

- Am not escalating the situation. No punishment or consequences are needed.
- Respect the student's food and body. I never want a student to be hungry on my account.
- Communicate that I believe in their best intentions. Should a student in eighth grade have known that ice cream wouldn't be the best choice to bring into class? Probably. But it's not worth damaging my relationship with them to shame them about it.
- Minimize the amount of class time that both the student and I miss.

Just know this: The only reason I know how to respond now is because of how many times I responded the wrong way earlier in my teaching. You won't do everything perfectly right. The teacher down the hall who seems to do everything perfectly spent a long time doing everything unperfectly. Every school day is full of uncertainties, but no matter how long you've been teaching, education is just an unpredictable gig. Embrace the hiccups and learn from them. You'll likely have a great story for later.

CHAPTER 6

Building Strong Bonds with Your Students

I had no idea I would struggle with building relationships with my students as a new teacher.

Right up until the day I started teaching, I equated building relationships with "getting kids to love me," which I was very good at. I was an all-star camp counselor, a highly sought-after babysitter, a glittering legend in various volunteer and mentoring opportunities with kids in my hometown and in nearby Houston. I'd never had to work for kids' affection or respect. It kind of just . . . happened. So although I knew the importance of building relationships with students in a vague sense, I waltzed into my first classroom convinced that my usual arsenal—a few jokes, asking kids a question or two about themselves, trying out a few games—was all I'd need. I was about to Mary Poppins my way into the Teaching Hall of Fame.

Spoiler alert: I did not.

There were the boundary-pushers who stood out in each class, yes, but I was also struggling with my classes as a whole. Teaching often felt like I was talking to a room full of strangers. And essentially they were. I didn't really know them the way I wanted to— not beyond names and maybe a couple of surface-level facts about each kid: This one has an older sister, this one plays basketball. But unlike some situations when strangers might do what you ask if it's been preestablished that you are the authority figure, in my classroom, I had practically no influence. If I asked for my students to take out a sheet of paper, it took multiple requests before anyone would even move. If I tried to build hype for a game I wanted them to play, everyone would drag their feet or roll their eyes. And in a school where administrators couldn't tell me what to do about students ignoring my directions, I was on my own to figure this out.

It didn't take long for me to realize just one of many reasons why teaching was so much harder than other roles I'd had with kids: I was in charge of making kids do something every day that they really, really didn't want to do. Unlike camp or babysitting, where the promise of pool time, snacks, or crafts was dangling like a carrot behind any not-fun task, here at school, the only incentive was learning, a process my students had been conditioned to dislike from years of not getting what they needed to be successful (small classes, resources, counselors, etc.). But even when I understood *why* my job was so hard, it would be years before I understood the power that building relationships has in alleviating the problem.

I think there's a misunderstanding among new teachers— and even among some veteran teachers—about what building relationships really means. The "relationships" chapters in a lot of teaching textbooks and online articles make it seem as if building relationships is a series of "one and done" things you can check off on your clipboard. "Have students fill out a survey about their favorite color, food, etc., at the beginning of the year." Check. "Ask your students about their interests." Check. "Ask your students how they're doing." Check. Ta-dah! They love you now!

While all of these *are* good ways to get to know your students, it's important to know that strong relationships cannot be reduced to a series of tasks. I know this because I *did* these tasks with my seventh graders in my first year of teaching, and yet I still didn't have the kind of solid, positive relationships I wanted in the classroom. That's because, if I'm being truly, painfully honest with myself, I didn't have the right motivation to get to know my students.

I thought I wanted positive relationships, but more than anything I wanted what I saw as the end result of having positive relationships: compliance.

I wanted to tell my class to get out a piece of paper and watch as twenty-eight bodies actually did it.

I wanted to announce that we were going to play a game and have everyone's full participation and enthusiasm.

I wanted teaching to not feel like a game of tug-of-war anymore.

Though my thinking was shortsighted, I don't think it was necessarily bad of me to want compliance. I genuinely wanted my students to leave my class loving the practice of reading and writing. What I didn't realize was that if I had done the right kind of work in building relationships with my students—treating them as people first and as learners second, I would have seen that compliance pops up as a side bonus to a whole slew of beautiful, magical, transformative things that happen when you really know the people you're teaching. Your job gets easier, yes, but your life connecting to the humanity in others gets infinitely richer.

When you build relationships with your students, you learn that the quiet boy, Anthony, in your class has a mother who is a classically trained cellist, and when she comes to Career Day and plays for your class you see him light up with pride. And suddenly, from then on, you see Anthony as more than a boy who is shy; you understand he is a person who has spent large parts of his childhood absorbing symphonies and operas from backstage while his peers were watching cartoons. You learn to teach the writing process to Anthony by using musical metaphors: restating your thesis is like returning to a coda; editing is like tuning.

You learn that Brianna, who has been unafraid to rile up her classmates since the first day of school, shares an apartment with seven siblings, including a little brother with special needs. You learn that while she doesn't want to talk about her personal life, she does want to read every book she can get her hands on that features a strong female lead taking down a dystopia, and you check in with her after every book she finishes. "What'd you think of the twist at the end?" "Did you know this is a trilogy?" "Who would you want to see cast in the movie?" And the Brianna that you used to see as disrupting your class is now a Brianna that you are convinced will do big things to help disrupt unfair systems.

Trust me. These kids—whether they're four years old or eighteen—are going to change your life. You might be great at building relationships with students from the get-go, or it may be a slower learning curve, but this area of teaching will inevitably be one of the more memorable aspects of your teaching career.

SEEN, HEARD, AND SAFE

When I think about the strongest relationships in my life, some core feelings come into mind. The people I'm the closest to and with whom I have the most meaningful relationships are people who make me feel:

- *Seen.* I feel like these people truly understand who I am— both at my best and at my worst—and love me no matter what kind of day I'm having. These people see and honor who I want to become and help hold me accountable in getting there.

- *Heard.* These people will always listen to what I have to say before jumping to conclusions. I feel heard in these relationships because these people act in a way that communicates that they understand what I've said, and they follow through by checking in on me later. I also feel like they make time to hear me because they want to, not because it's an obligation.

- *Safe.* I can trust these people to tell me the truth about myself, and I can trust that these people have my best interests at heart. I know because their actions have proven over time that they don't have an agenda to harm or manipulate me.

This is what relationships are, and these ought to be our goals with our students, too: to communicate to them with appropriate professional boundaries that we see them, we hear them, and that they are safe with us. When you build relationships with students, these three things should be the driving force, or muscle, behind your actions.

What does it look like to have this "muscle"?

In brief: It's never a shortcut. It's never the easy way out. It's never a "one and done." Building relationships with your students—just like any other relationships you have in your life—is an ongoing process that takes work. It takes heart.

So what does this muscle look like?

Let's look at a seventh-grade teacher giving her students a beginning-of-the-year survey on the first day. A teacher who might not understand the nuances in relationship-building might find a premade questionnaire online with basic questions about a student's favorite foods, favorite colors, etc., and print it out for her classes without changing anything. She might read over her students' responses that night, and then let the questionnaires sit in a drawer for the rest of the year. This teacher might occasionally remember one or two "standouts"—the student who likes the same video game she does, or the student who wrote "IDK" for half of his answers.

With a teacher who knows that building relationships takes muscle, however, the approach would be much different. This teacher might find a premade questionnaire online with basic questions, but will add several questions to the survey after asking herself, "Okay, what do I *really* want to know about my students? What kind of questions will begin to tell me who they are?" The teacher will add questions that show her more about her students than simply asking them their favorite color. Questions like:

Tell me how you feel about science. (It's okay if you've never liked it before!)

Would you rather find yourself in a field with one horse-sized duck, or one hundred duck-sized horses? Explain your answer.

This teacher will pore over her students' responses, and use them almost like flash cards, until she has an emerging sense of who each student is. Then, she can use this information in individual conversations with students over the next several weeks. Here are a few examples: "Hey, I noticed on your survey you said you're in a *ballet folklorico* group (a traditional dance from Mexico that is popular in Houston). Tell me more about that!" or "I loved your response to my question about your favorite person—your aunt sounds so brave." She makes a point to check in with each student at least once before the end of the first three weeks.

Both of these teachers have made a good choice in giving their students an interests survey the first day of school—but one teacher treated it as the finish line, where the other treated it as the starting point. Your work in building relationships as a teacher is an everyday task. This can seem daunting in a profession where the workload is already sky-high, but when you're a skilled relationship builder, you'll see how connecting with your students doesn't feel like work at all.

Below are some easy (and free!) ways of building relationships with your students in each of the "seen, heard, and safe" categories:

SHOWING YOUR STUDENTS THEY ARE SEEN

— **Greet students at the door each day.** I touched on this in the previous chapter, but it's worth mentioning a second time. Though it might feel easy to write off in a school day where every minute counts, it is a research-proven way of increasing student engagement and improving the teacher-student relationship. Here are some specific ways you can show students you "see" them from the moment they cross your path.

— **Have a quick verbal check-in periodically.** Tell students who were absent the day before, "We missed you! I'm so glad you're back." This can also be time for a superquick chat with a student about the final score in last night's sportsball game, admiring a student's cat socks, wishing them a happy Rosh Hashanah or Eid al-Fitr, etc.

— **Scan students' faces for concerning changes in mood or appearance.** If you sense things might be off, use your discretion to decide whether a quick "Hey, everything okay?" is appropriate or whether it would be better to follow up in a private conversation later.

— **Consider more "creative" greetings.** Elementary students might appreciate rotating roles for a "class greeter" who stands beside you at the entrance to your classroom. Or consider letting your students decide how they want to be greeted. You can find signs online (search "class greeting signs") with options—high five, handshake, dancing, etc. Now that I think about it, my eighth graders would probably love this. We just might never get class started.

Or maybe you'll think of your own signature greeting method. I will never forget a reader who sent me a picture of her greeting students while wearing a muscle-y, green foam Hulk arm that she uses to fist-bump or politely shake hands with each student who enters the room. I'm not saying you couldn't come to class angry after fist-bumping the Hulk . . . but it would be pretty hard.

— **Go to students' games, performances, and other events.** Participate in special events that they are part of outside of the classroom, and be sure to connect with them afterward. If you can't catch the student immediately after the event, follow up the next time you see the student in class to say what a great job they did and the parts that stood out to you. I like to make goofy signs for my students' events that I can reuse for future events, such as this orchestra poster.[1]

— **Use encouragement whenever possible.** Rather than focus on praise (which can set up the perfectionists in our classroom to have an unhealthy dependence on achievement),[2] make sure to recognize and encourage hard work, persistence, and progress when you see it. It may be something academic—"I'm so proud of you for sticking with quadratic

---

1 Get it? Orca-straw? One of my students, upon seeing it for the first time, said, "You love whale juice?"

2 Raising my own hand here.

equations!" Or it could be related to a student's behavior or character—"How great did it feel leaving the library cleaner than we found it?" This doesn't mean you can't congratulate your students on their successes, but focusing positive recognition on the process instead of the end result fosters independence and the importance of trying even when you *don't* get recognized for it.

— **Know what drives each of your students.** Ask your students questions that go beyond what teachers typically ask at the beginning of the school year, such as "What do you want to be when you grow up?" or "What are your goals for this school year?" If you stick with these generic prompts, you are likely to get manufactured, passionless responses. Instead, once you have built a classroom environment where students feel safe and supported, find out what is truly important to them, right now, today. What problem in the world would they most want to solve? What is their prized possession(s)? What culture would they most love to learn about? What people, ideas, or causes are they the fiercest about protecting? Where do they see themselves in ten years? Twenty?

SHOWING YOUR STUDENTS THEY ARE HEARD

— **Check in with students regularly via journaling and/or conferences.** We would all love to have the time to have deep conversations with our students every day, but that can be a tough thing to do when you have large class sizes and a lot of curriculum to cover. Two strategies I'd recommend:

1. **Journaling.** When I taught my largest classes, I asked students to answer three or four very short journal

prompts for homework every few days and then turn these journals in once every two weeks. Though these journals gave my students a chance to practice writing, these were not academic assignments. Sometimes I would ask what they thought about current events or pose a funny "Would you rather . . ." question, but one question in the set was always "How are things going right now?" When I would "grade" the journals, I would make sure to respond to *every entry*, even if it was just a smiley face next to something I liked, or "Good point!" or "This is awesome!" I would write a short, two- or three-sentence note at the end about how good it was to hear from them, and occasionally I would write a letter back. Compared to other things I would grade, these hardly took any time at all and were 100 percent worth it to strengthen the relationships I was forming with my students.

2. **Conferences.** This strategy might work better with smaller class sizes or in classes that are skilled at working independently, but don't be afraid to try it! Over the course of anywhere from a week to a month, make it a point to check in with each student one-on-one, either in a quiet corner of your class or in the hallway (with your door open to keep an eye on your other students). I recommend starting with "How are things going right now?" which gives your student the low-risk option of talking about how things are going in class, but also the option to tell you about other things outside of school they may be excited about or struggling with.

— **Get feedback from your students on what's working in class and what isn't.** You can do this in a number of ways. You can ask individual students or small groups; poll students in person or through written surveys; have them use pencil and paper or a Google form or other online form. Regardless of which format you choose, you'll want to give students an opportunity to talk about what they already like and what they see has room for improvement—when it comes to both their learning and your teaching. Doing this shows students that you recognize the importance of their voice and actually want to hear from them.

There's only one rule with asking for feedback as a teacher: You can't get mad about what students choose to tell you ☺. If you hand out surveys, at least one of your students is bound to either not take it seriously or leave you a scathing review, whether or not it's deserved. Consider these responses an indication of the relationships (and teaching methods) you need to improve, not a personal attack.

— **Make changes in your class based on student feedback.** After you get feedback from students, follow up with your classes about all the great information you got and thank them for showing you how you can improve. Tell them the changes you plan to make and establish a future checkpoint for following up with your students. Note: Obviously if half of your fourth-grade language arts students report that they don't like having to read, you're not going to eliminate all reading. But use this as an opportunity for further inquiry. What *about* reading in your class do they not like? What would make reading better? Choosing their own books? Having a wider selection? A quieter reading environment?

SHOWING YOUR STUDENTS THEY ARE SAFE

— **Apologize when you miss the mark.** This is so important for students to feel like they're in good hands. Model good leadership by taking ownership of your mistakes in the classroom—because they will happen—and apologizing for them. Good leaders know that apologizing to children isn't weak; insisting you're above apologizing to children is.

— **Make it abundantly clear that your room is a safe space for *all* students.** Your actions will show you treat all students fairly more than words ever could, but it is still an important point to make directly. For students who face microaggressive or direct discrimination because of race, sexuality, religion, or other factors related to their personhood, it can be a huge relief to know that their teacher is not only going to treat them fairly, but will be on the lookout to make sure other students are treating them fairly, too. At the beginning of the school year, on my list of procedures and policies, I have this statement: *This classroom is safe.* I explain to students what I mean with something like, "There are a lot of places where it's not okay to be who you are. There are a lot of places where someone might give you a bad label because of what you believe, or assume negative things about you because of something you can't help, or not give you the same opportunities as other people because of who you like. This is not one of those places. We are all wildly, beautifully different people, and we will never accomplish what we want to do if someone doesn't feel safe to be who they are. This doesn't just mean that I'm the watchdog for discrimination—we all have to be watchdogs in here to make this a safe place. What questions do you have about this?"

— **Educate yourself on issues that affect the population you teach and the community you serve.** Ask your principal about what issues tend to most affect the population you teach and start reading about it, *especially if this community is very different from the one where you grew up or currently live.* Depending on the community, these issues could be things like poverty, suicide, racism, LGBTQ discrimination, Islamophobia, drug usage, the school-to-prison pipeline, absenteeism, family alcoholism—it's a long, long list. With any issue affecting your students, seek to understand and listen to the voices in that community above everything else, and seek to deconstruct biases you may hold. Students are very perceptive and can tell very quickly whether your intentions are genuine or if you just have a savior mentality and your own rigid opinions on how to "fix" what's broken. Accept the possibility that your viewpoints—ones you've held your whole life—might change. You cannot and will not build relationships with people you think you're above.

We've talked about how great relationships between teachers and students can be built, but I think it's important to acknowledge the types of relationships and situations teachers should try to avoid, too. We've all heard news headlines about the *really* bad apples in the teaching profession, but there are plenty of ways that relationships with students can be dysfunctional, questionable, or flawed without being illegal. If you want to know how to do relationships the right way, sometimes you also have to know how to avoid doing things the wrong way.

Teacher vs. Friend

Eventually in teaching, you'll hear a teacher say something along the lines of, "I'm their teacher, not their friend." This refers to the dualistic notion that you can either be a teacher who gets things done, or someone who cares about their students on a social-emotional level.

But like most black-and-white choices, I reject the idea that we have to choose between being an effective teacher or someone who cares about students as people. We can be both! I like to think that we should aim for the middle in the sliding scale below:

I'm their teacher, period.

My job is to teach—that's it.
I don't care whether students like me.
Relationships shouldn't matter in the teaching world.
I don't have favorite students.
I consider my students an extension of my job, nothing more.

The middle!

My job is to teach, but I teach human beings with complex inner lives and emotions, so part of my job *is* caring about them as people.
I don't let my students' temporary emotions or opinions of me shake me, but I also know that their experience in my class matters to me because research tells us that students who want to be there do better.
I have students I connect with more easily (I'm human!), but I make a concerted effort to make sure they don't get special treatment or disproportionate attention—it's important to me that *all* my students see a model of equitable treatment.

> **I'm their buddy at all costs!**
>
> My students must like me and vice versa.
> I would be annoyed and personally offended if I found out
> one of my students didn't like me or my class.
> I definitely have favorites and my students know it.
> Being the "cool" teacher is more important to me than being
> the best teacher I can be.
> I consider my students my friends.

A SHORT LIST OF THINGS YOU SHOULDN'T DO WHEN BUILDING RELATIONSHIPS WITH STUDENTS:

— **Don't give students your personal cell number.** While I see the good intention here and the usefulness of a student having a teacher's cell phone number in certain emergencies (especially if the student has a lack of resources at home), ultimately I think it is a better idea to make sure your students have access to emergency numbers that don't put you, your job, and your information at risk. There are too many apps out there that can manufacture fake texts, too many programs and services students could register with using your phone number, too many ways your well-intentioned offer could result in a disaster.

— **Don't engage in inappropriate conversations.** Your district should have mandatory training on where "the line" is, but a good rule of thumb is to not talk about anything that you wouldn't want a screenshot of on the local news the following day. You can always refer a student to a counselor or mental health expert for consultation that goes beyond the realm of your expertise as a teacher.

(Note: Make sure to keep a record of counselor referrals in case your documentation is needed later.)

— **Don't hang with students outside of school.** I know some teachers who serve in other community roles and spend time with students in structured time through churches, community sports or theater, or other organizations, and this is completely fine. But inviting students to hang out (or accepting invitations to hang out), even in a public place, is not a good idea. It invites suspicion, rumors, gossip—all of which can be damaging to your personal and professional reputation. There should be no reason that students who want to talk to you can't do so at school.

— **Don't help a group of eighth graders come up with a "Who's Hot and Who's Not" list of students in their grade.**[3]

Though I treasure the relationships I have with my students now, learning how to build meaningful relationships was a slow learning process. Every year I've navigated through changes I've needed to make in my own approach to connecting with the people in my classroom, especially in the constant process of examining myself and my teaching for cultural bias. You'll make mistakes that will set you back, like punishing the whole class because you're not sure who carved the words "fuck Baked Lays" into a desk when you had a sub. You'll get frustrated at times that no matter how fiercely you love your students, the results aren't always in your control and don't operate under your timeline.

---

3   Someone I worked with did this—don't worry, she's no longer a teacher. But note to legislators who may be reading this book: These are the kind of teachers you attract when you respond to teacher shortages by *lowering the standards to become a teacher* instead of improving conditions for your existing pool of talented teachers. Thank you for coming to my TED Talk.

But with anything, we get better by acknowledging where we fall short and by *doing better*. Trying and failing and apologizing and getting back up and making changes to make things right: this is how any relationship gets better, and it works the same in teaching. I can guarantee you this (and there are so few things in this book I can guarantee): You will never regret the work you put in to connect with your students.

CHAPTER 7

Instruction: What to Do About the *NOTHING I'M DOING IS WORKING!* Feeling

Whenever I have a student teacher or I am mentoring someone new to teaching on our campus, I like to tell a story from my first year of teaching. It's a story about hope. About failure. And about a stranger named Paul.

Let me tell you a tale about Limerick Day.

By early November of my first year, after two months of teaching lessons that were the educational equivalent of flaming bags of garbage, I decided to do something different. With every lesson I tried, it seemed like I had to stop halfway through and find an alternative way of teaching it, abandon the lesson altogether because it was taking too long, or the content was completely wiped from my students' brains by the next day.[1] My most carefully laid plans would sputter and die when I tried to put them into action. I was tired of feeling like a failure, and I knew my students deserved better than what I was giving them. So, one day while I was typing up lesson plans for the following week, though it wasn't in the district's recommended curriculum plan, I decided to set aside one whole day for a fun, laid-back lesson: teaching students to write limericks.

You know what limericks are, right? Those five-line poems with a really strong rhythm and rhyming pattern that usually start with something along the lines of, "There once was a (something) named (something)?" Many of the popular limericks are bawdy,[2] but there are plenty of school-appropriate ones, too, like the "Two Cats of Kilkenny," or "Hickory Dickory Dock."[3]

Anyway, Limerick Day was going to be awesome. I knew limericks weren't exactly as rigorous as some of my other lessons, but it would be fun, I'd have my students engaging with language in a creative way, and, most important, it would be easy. My students needed to feel successful. I needed to feel successful. I visualized my cold, lifeless classroom abuzz with excitement, laughing as they clapped out syllables and crafted their

---

1   My fault, by the way—not my students'. They were forgetting what I taught them a day later because I didn't teach to mastery. Read on in this chapter for more on this topic.

2   You probably have an uncle John who has, like, fifteen of this kind memorized.

3   If you have no idea what I'm talking about, you need to stop right here and go buy Richard Scarry's *Best Mother Goose Ever* for your social-emotional education.

own limericks. They would be participating! Engaged! Actively learning!

I built Limerick Day up big-time. I put a countdown on the board in big green letters with four-leaf clovers and encouraged students not to be absent on Friday. I created a PowerPoint with memes, fun limericks, and little animations that broke down limericks into rhyme schemes, gave examples I handpicked because they were hilarious, and had a template labeled with how many syllables each line should have. In my notes for the PowerPoint, I had an amazing joke ready that I knew was going to slay. Part of my lesson plan was to build in time for willing students to share their limericks, and I set aside twenty minutes for this because obviously everyone would want to share. I even bought little prizes for first, second, and third place! Just because!

Limerick Day was the savior we needed.

As you might have been able to guess from the heavy-handed foreshadowing, Limerick Day was a disaster. I realized very quickly into my lesson that my students didn't have much of the prior knowledge needed to successfully write limericks. Very few of them knew how to count out the syllables in a word (and I realized I didn't know how else to teach counting syllables beyond the clap-it-out method). When I asked students for an example of a word that rhymed with *singing* a lone hand went up after ten seconds with the response, ". . . Driving?"

By this point in the year, I knew how much the opportunity and resource gaps in education had stunted my students. When property taxes fund schools, students born in zip codes with lower property values don't get educational resources that are equitable to those of their wealthier peers; as a result, they are often behind in literacy. I had considered that maybe my

students wouldn't know or had forgotten the definition of a sylla-
ble, but I figured they could still identify and manipulate them.
(I mean, think about it—most adults probably can't define a sub-
ordinating conjunction, but they still use them every day.) I had
no idea how behind my students were on simple fundamentals.

Suddenly, right there in the middle of Limerick Day, I realized I was feeling a lot of things. I was frustrated at myself for not
anticipating that my students couldn't complete this lesson. I was
mad at the system that let my students get to seventh grade without knowing rhyming words. And I was crushed thinking about
what it would look like to my students if I abruptly switched to a
new activity. It's not that they were having the time of their lives,
but I knew my students were smart—they wouldn't see the sudden abandonment of Limerick Day as a strategic pedagogical
move like I did; they would think: *She just figured out we're too dumb
for this.* Not to mention that this early in my teaching, I didn't
have any ready-to-go lessons in my repertoire to fall back on.

And so, I made the executive decision to forge ahead with
Limerick Day.

I gave them all worksheets to practice writing limericks, and
almost instantly had a room full of raised hands, with questions
or comments such as, "Miss, I don't know any words that rhyme
with *wolf,*"[4] and "This is too hard," and "How many syllables are
in *orange?*"[5]

Sensing that I was losing them, I decided to try out my joke.
Maybe we were struggling, but we could at least laugh.

"Whatever you do," I said, slowly for effect, "make sure your
first line isn't, *There once was a man from Nantucket!*"

---

4   I didn't and still don't.
5   One? Two? No clue.

Silence. Then:

"Is that by Dallas?"

We were flatlining. Students who waited for too long with raised hands began fidgeting, tattooing themselves with markers, and folding their worksheets into fortune-tellers. My students who were further along in rhyming were reciting inventive lines with words rhyming with *grass*, *witch*, and *luck*.

"I thought this was supposed to be fun?" I overheard one frustrated student say.

"Oh . . . sorry," she said sheepishly, meeting my eyes, which I imagine looked like a sad bassett hound's.

Limerick Day for my other classes went similarly. Class after class, I watched as the genuine effort and excitement I'd put into Limerick Day spectacularly crashed and burned to the ground.

At the end of the day, completely crestfallen, I gathered up the worksheets I had collected and sat down at a student desk to go through them, hoping to find some kind of evidence that even a shred of my instruction had stuck. Flipping through the stack I saw that the first dozen or so worksheets weren't even finished, they had been abandoned by or near the midway point. But finally, I made it to a worksheet that looked completed, and with a tiny sparkle of hope in my heart, noticed that there was a neat, five-line poem at the end in the space I'd marked "Write your own limerick here!" I smiled. Then I read the words I would never forget.

> *There once was a boy from Texas*
> *Who smelled very hick-y*
> *He felt rain on his body*
> *As he got a clean shower*
> *I'll see you later, Paul.*

"Paul?" I whispered out loud.

I was frustrated that Limerick Day was a total bust, yes, but the real reason I lost it was bigger than that. Limerick Day was only the most recent in what had been a long parade of failed lessons. It seemed that the more effort I put in, the greater the disaster and the greater my disappointment. At no other point in my life had hard work and a positive attitude not resulted in what I wanted.

From the depths of my soul, it seemed, a cry was echoing louder and louder.

Nothing I'm doing is working.

"Nothing I'm doing is working" is a secret thought that, right at this moment, I would guess tens of thousands of teachers are thinking but are terrified to admit to anyone else. They carry this secret to faculty meetings, to planning meetings with their team, to dinner with their family and friends. They can't say it out loud, because how disturbing is it for someone else to hear that you are *failing America's children?*

Having been in that headspace myself, I will tell you that the "Nothing I'm doing is working" feeling doesn't feel like an exaggeration. On Limerick Day and on many, many other days in my rookie years, I believed that nothing I did was working.

Nothing I've done has reached my students or been retained by them.

My teaching is completely ineffective.

Everyone else is better at this than me.

My students are going to plummet into the abyss one at a time, like lemmings over a cliff, and it's all my fault.

The first piece of good news is this: It's not true. "Nothing I'm doing is working" is a false narrative (more about this in chapter 13). You are not destroying anyone's future. I can rattle off a whole list of people who have been elected to protect and secure the future of America's children and who truly are doing the worst job imaginable, but you are not among them. You are out here in the trenches, working hard in the best way you know how, learning more every damn day. *You are not failing America's children.* Clap out that sentence if you want. (It's eleven syllables.)

The other piece of good news is that there are so many ways to improve your instruction. This is one of the few areas of teaching where I do think the literature out there is helpful, because best practices in pedagogy are best practices anywhere, no matter who, where, or what you teach. There are resources that outline strategies in providing feedback to students, holding effective classroom discussions, teaching students to be aware of their own learning through metacognition. They are the kind of practices you will see happening in the classrooms of talented teachers in every kind of classroom imaginable. Some activities might require stronger classroom management or work better in small classes, but there's no reason you can't adapt best practices to incorporate wherever you teach. And if you're thinking, *But I learned about all of that in my teaching training?* I would strongly recommend going back and rereading. I'm betting your classroom in real life is very different from the classroom you had in your head when you were reading your teaching books. Sometimes I think teaching certification should be backward—first you student teach, THEN you start learning how it all works.[6]

---

6   Patent pending on the Love, Teach method of Backward Teaching Certification.

Before I get to my tips, please remember that I do not purport to be any kind of pedagogical guru. While much of the following is similar to or based on existing best practices (many of which are from experts), these are simply things I've learned that have worked for me. Have I worked in a range of schools and grades and am I familiar with the demands of teaching right now? Yes. Does this mean these strategies will work for everyone? No. Please don't hesitate to ask around (it's particularly important to talk to teachers in your school or district, who will know your students better than anyone), read up on research-based strategies, or discover your own solutions.

Even though classroom management and instruction are very closely linked, I personally think it's much quicker and easier to see improvement in instruction than in a more nebulous, less predictable area like classroom management. While it's difficult for me to pin down what I did to improve my classroom management or exact moments where my classroom management changed, I can easily rattle off instructional changes I implemented—either from trainings, literature, or my own guesswork—that resulted in meaningful, sometimes immediate changes for my students.

When it comes to the big, overwhelming "Nothing I'm Doing Is Working" feeling, we can usually break it down into one or more of the following problems, each of which I've personally struggled with.

THE STANDARDS I'M EXPECTED TO TEACH ARE WAY TOO ADVANCED FOR MY STUDENTS

I cried about this approximately sixty-five times my first year. It can feel extremely overwhelming to be working with kids who are behind through no fault of their own, especially in a school lacking access to resources. But had I truly understood some of the following concepts that first year, I would have done a lot less crying and my students would have done a lot more learning.

First, Abandon a Deficit Mind-Set

If you're constantly focusing on what your students can't do, it will be really hard for you or your students to ever celebrate (or even make) progress. And I'll be the first to tell you that it was really hard for me as a new teacher to do this. I wanted evidence on paper—essays, test scores—that my students were just as brilliant and capable as students in schools with the best funding. The problem was not that my students weren't as brilliant or capable, it was that I was expecting to see that kind of evidence in a single school year. After several years as a teacher, I learned that making absolute perfection my goal wasn't good for me or my students.

Instead, I continued to keep my expectations high, but I learned to treasure, flip out over, and be thrilled about progress. Taking a student from 20 percent mastery of concepts at the beginning of the year to 67 percent in May might look like failure if you're in a deficit mind-set, but if you have learned to love progress? *Dang*. Forty-seven percent growth in ONE YEAR? Think about how much this student can grow with next year's teacher if they're starting out this much further ahead! This is absolutely something to celebrate.

"Where can we go from here?" is a much better question than "How will we ever get to where we need to be?" "Look at the improvement toward our goal!" is a much healthier observation than "Look how far we have to go still!" Save the miserable wallowing for thinking about unqualified secretaries of education or something actually wallow-worthy. We have work to do.

Plan Backward and Use Scaffold Learning

You've likely learned about backward planning in your certification, but I'm willing to bet you didn't anticipate just how far backward you'd have to go or how little time you'd have to do it. For those of you who don't know, backward planning involves starting by looking at the ideal outcome—what does mastery look like at the end of this unit?—and working backward. From the assessment you can create a list of ALL the skills kids will need in order to master the unit. Once you have all the skills together in a list, you can create a diagnostic exam to figure out which of those skills your students already know. *Exam* sounds like a sit-down pretest, which it can be, or it can be as simple as a survey or class discussion. Then, once you know where they are and where they need to be, you can plan out the unit by scaffolding the learning into chunks that build toward mastery.

Let's say you're the culinary arts teacher and you want your students to be able to make a grilled cheese sandwich. You begin by planning your ending *assessment,* a sandwich that 1) has golden-brown, buttery sides; 2) is completely melted all the way through its cheesy middle; and 3) tastes delicious. To get there, you don't just say, okay, I'm going to have each student grab supplies and just start. Instead, you list all the skills required to make a sandwich with those qualities. To be successful at the end of this unit, students will need to know:

- how to use a stove and knife safely
- how to measure and use kitchen measuring equipment
- common cooking abbreviations, including *T.* and *t.*
- how to use a cheese grater
- how to spread butter (softened, not chilled)

- how to assess grilled bread from a visual standpoint, i.e., what *underdone* or *burned* looks like
- which types of cheese are best for grilled cheese sandwiches
- the right stove temperature for a grilled cheese sandwich
- the correct pan for a grilled cheese sandwich
- when and how to flip

Once you have the list of skills assembled, you can start determining what students already know. Maybe you create a diagnostic exam with pretest questions like "Which of the following stove settings is best for a grilled cheese sandwich?" Or maybe you ask students in a survey to list the steps they think are necessary in making a grilled cheese sandwich. Maybe your diagnostic reveals that students know absolutely nothing about grilled cheese sandwiches and it's a good thing you checked, or maybe they know everything except the best cheeses to use and you can jump straight to that step, but either way, you can start your instruction where the students are already instead of guessing.

If I had backward-planned correctly, I would have known my students weren't ready to write limericks because I would have checked the skills necessary to be successful in advance: rhyming, breaking down syllables, maintaining rhythm, etc.

Don't be afraid to start small with your steps in building to the end assessment. When your students don't know the basics, it can feel overwhelming going backward twenty steps to address those first. But think about it this way: If you've never run a marathon before, you're not going to go out your first day of training and try to run 26.2 miles. Instead, you probably will follow a carefully planned, incremented regimen that starts with a few miles at first and then gradually builds. In the same way, you can't expect to teach students how to write a research paper in a single class period—you have to break it up and drill down to the basics, like how to write a transition sentence, for example. Which brings me to my next point.[7]

Try Not to Be Daunted by the Academic Calendar

It can be really intimidating to look at an academic calendar and realize you will need way more time to give your kids the essential knowledge and skills for your content area than what you've been provided.

My "professional" advice is to align yourself with your district's calendar.

My actual advice is to use the academic calendar as a guide, but when it comes to absolute fundamentals like students being able to *read* and *write* and *add* and *think*—things that will undoubtedly make meeting their other learning standards much easier for the rest of the year—customize your schedule to focus your time as needed. You may be off by a few days or have to change your plans a bit (or a lot), but forging ahead with an ambitious academic calendar knowing that your students will have fundamental gaps in their learning is irresponsible. It's also irresponsible of districts to demand that you do this.

Here's an example of how I've used an academic calendar loosely. When I taught a resource class for students who had literacy challenges, I looked at the short story unit on our district's academic calendar and saw that over the course of a ten-day unit, it required students to read five to six short stories, and some were assigned as homework. I knew my students' reading levels

---

7 See what I did there? Did you roll your eyes? Good.

and stamina from formal and informal assessments I'd done, and I knew that the pace and volume weren't right for them. I also knew that assigning any reading as homework would put any students who didn't do the reading even further behind when they came to class.

So this is what that ten-day unit ended up looking like in my class:

- Three full class days devoted to building vocabulary, short story terms, and concepts related to fiction
- One full class day of building anticipation for the first short story with pre-reading activities and cementing the historical/cultural context
- Two full class days reading the first short story in class, stopping occasionally to model good reading practices like questioning or predicting, and using short story vocabulary and concepts we'd practiced
- One full class day of building anticipation for the second short story
- Two full class days reading the second short story in class
- One full class day having students compare the stories in discussion using the vocabulary and terms we'd been using as well as the historical/cultural contexts
- Half a class day reviewing what we learned, half with an assessment of their learning

Yes, that's eleven days. Yes, I was behind a day. Yes, we read two stories instead of six. But instead of blazing through five to six short stories that my students weren't quite ready for just then, we spent that time reading two handpicked short stories with depth and complexity, while establishing good reading practices. Most importantly, I was able to let my students feel the joy of reading something great and actually understanding it. Maybe I didn't get 100 percent mastery on the assessment, but all of my students *passed*, and I guarantee you that I got way better results than if I had blindly followed the district calendar.

I know that some districts expect all teachers to be teaching the exact same thing on the exact same day using the exact same resources, but that is so professionally insulting and culturally unresponsive that it makes my head hurt. Again, my "professional" advice if you're in a district like this is to follow your district calendar. But my actual advice depends on whether you have an understanding appraiser who is well-informed on best practices. If you do, sit down with them, show them your detailed plans for that unit, and explain how your way will also get students learning with depth and complexity and fill in crucial gaps in their learning that you've noticed. If your principal is not well-informed on best practices, say nothing about your plans, and if they come in your room and ask why you're not reading what Ms. Applegate is reading next door, feign ignorance and say you mixed up your lessons.

Of course, if they continue to come in and micromanage your teaching and ask you to follow plans that continue to leave your students behind, you'll need to make some professional decisions. But we have to do what's best for kids, especially when the people in charge of doing what's best for kids won't.

MY LESSONS JUST AREN'T WORKING

As you can clearly see from my Limerick Day disaster, when it comes to feeling like your lessons are going nowhere, *I have been there*. You may hear some teachers say that their lessons aren't working because of some kind of outside force—the students themselves, their families, the school's resources. Don't get me wrong; these things absolutely have an impact on student learning. But at the end of the day, you have to understand that the only thing you DO have control over is you. You can improve your instruction, but only if you're willing to be vulnerable and accept the idea that you need to improve your instruction.

(FYI: All teachers, not just new teachers, can improve their instruction. If you hear a teacher saying that they don't need improvement, file that kind of attitude away as an attitude you do not want to emulate.)

Here are some things you may want to consider trying if you find that your lessons keep failing or your students aren't retaining them.

Assess Whether Your Classroom Management May Be Playing a Role

If you are pretty convinced that your lesson plans are strong— either because you're working closely with a veteran teacher or using district-approved resources that are appropriate for the students you teach—consider the possibility that classroom management or the climate of your class may be playing a bigger role in the learning happening in your room. You may need to tighten up your procedures or develop more positive relationships with your classes to see the kind of learning you want to happen.

You May Not Be Teaching What You Think

What tends to happen often with new teachers is that they'll think they're teaching one thing, but the activities and resources they're using are insufficient. For example, this is one of the learning standards for third-grade reading in my state:

6A: Describe the characteristics of various forms of poetry and how they create imagery (e.g., narrative poetry, lyrical poetry, humorous poetry, free verse).

Some teachers might design lessons that have students:
-Define each of the different types of poetry
-Read different examples of each type of poetry, or
-Identify the kind of poem from a given selection

These are all great activities, especially as stepping-stones to get to the eventual standard, but none of these activities actually ask students to describe the characteristics of different types of poetry or how they create imagery. Students might be able to define free verse perfectly but get totally stumped when an assessment asks, *How does this poem create an image in the reader's mind?* That's because students had practice reading, defining, and identifying a lyrical poem but no practice describing how a lyrical poem is using imagery to paint a mental picture. At some point in your teaching of a concept in your unit, you must make sure your students are performing exactly what the standard asks—and nothing less. It's important to know that aligning what your students are doing in class to state standards is not about "teaching to the test," it's about making sure you're not falling short when it comes to having high expectations for your students.

Try to Repeat Exposure to Concepts Through Warm-Ups, Mini-Lessons, and Anchor Charts
Sometimes it's not a matter of your lesson itself being ineffective but simply that your students need more exposure and practice. While you can't always devote several weeks to a lesson that was

supposed to last two, you can reinforce concepts in a variety of ways. If you notice that students still need practice on a certain skill, try these ideas:

POST one or two questions on that topic as warm-up questions on the board at the beginning of each class period for several weeks.

REVISIT these concepts in five- or ten-minute mini-lessons instead of whole lessons or class periods.

REINFORCE skills with videos students are expected to watch outside of class (if students have access to phones and/or Wi-Fi).

HANG anchor charts, or charts that reinforce learning through visuals, around the classroom so students can quickly access info they have trouble remembering (e.g., when to use an apostrophe with plural words or what the steps of the scientific method are).

Have a Talented Veteran Coworker or a District Expert Observe Your Planning/Teaching

This is a great option for when you're completely stumped on why your lessons aren't working, and something I think all teachers should be doing more often—not just newer teachers. Often, another teacher can point out things you have completely missed or have never considered. And if they're truly good at what they do, they will also point out what you're doing right (which, if you're like me, are also things you may never have considered).

MY KIDS AREN'T PAYING ATTENTION

I personally haven't dealt with this issue before, but I'll try to imagine what it's like to have students who don't think all my lessons are engaging and dynamic.

Hahahahaha. Just kidding. Once during my second year, an administrator told me after an observation that my lesson was so boring he fell asleep. So there's that. (In my defense, he was such a tyrannical leader that his presence in my room made me freeze up and behave like a malfunctioning robot. But also my teaching wasn't great. More on that in chapter 13.)

Here are some things that I've picked up along the way or learned from other teachers to get kids a little more onto the fully conscious side in your classroom:

Come up with a killer hook. Think about ways to draw your students in to your upcoming unit or lesson in a way that will definitely get their attention. Visuals are powerful, such as a thought-provoking quote or message on the board. You can also rearrange or redecorate the room to tie in to a topic, or dress up as a character. Another idea is to play around with sound effects or music; a professor I had in college started each class by playing great modern songs connected to themes from the previous night's reading.

Do be careful, however, to make sure that the way you engage students remains respectful to all groups, especially ones that are marginalized. Do not attempt to make lessons on the Trail of Tears or slave auctions "more fun" by acting them out or reducing them to insulting comparisons. You can engage students and build authentic interest without gamifying tragedy.

Spend time talking about the "why." We've all learned in certification that students need to understand the relevance of their learning. But my students (and I) got real tired, real fast of repeating over and over that they needed a skill for this standardized test or that class in high school. It was way more effective when we got to the heart of the matter. Why does it matter to read stories about people who are different from us? Why—even if college isn't something we're interested in—should we know how to read and analyze nonfiction writing? What value does writing have apart from academics? Because these can be tough questions, I have my students jot down ideas in journals for the first one to two minutes of class, then chat with a partner or group about it before we discuss as a class.

Make them talk and/or walk. Students retain much more information if they talk about what they're learning instead of just writing or listening (this is called the *production effect*). Although my primary and elementary teaching friends tell me that whole-class read-alouds are super effective, at the middle school level I find them very children-of-the-corn-like. Instead, I like to have students repeat small bits of information—grammar rules, new vocabulary, the acronym RAVEN for remembering the difference between "affect" and "effect"[8]—several times as different people: a cowboy, a drill sergeant,[9] or Moaning Myrtle from the *Harry Potter* series. They don't realize they're cementing knowledge in their head and I get to hear their terrible attempts at British accents, so we both win. Another strategy is creating structured conversations. Post a sentence

---

8   Remember: Affect-Verb, Effect-Noun!
9   Maybe check with the teacher(s) you share a wall with to see if it's a good day to bring out the drill-sergeant voices.

stem, like "One example of a chemical reaction is _____" and tell students they have two minutes to repeat this with five different partners while balancing on one leg or while half of the class is doing wall sits. It's impossible to zone out when you're switching things up so quickly.

Change the way you check for understanding. If you always (or even often) use the same method to check whether students understood your lesson or not, consider changing things up every once in a while. Consider asking your students to:

Write a "Twitter post" in a journal that describes what they've learned and have them keep it under 140 characters. Choose a different one every day to post on a class account (check first with your district's policies on social media).

Submit a draft for a class blog entry for the day.

Use technology like Padlet to post ideas on a collective online document.

Make a foldable or visual model/diagram to demonstrate what they've learned. (I didn't learn about foldables until year three—google them!)

Write on mini dry-erase boards to show you their answer as a class, but only with a very firm procedure in place about how they should be used and what will happen if they choose to draw *anything unrelated to the lesson on them.*

Write a letter to next year's students explaining what
they're about to learn, what was difficult for them,
and include tips on studying.

It took a while, but eventually I recovered from the pedagogical funeral pyre known as Limerick Day. A few months later,
once the ashes had cooled, I planned another fun day for my
students, but decided on a different lesson: haikus.

This time, I had my students in mind while planning. I thought
about what they knew already (syllables, now, thanks to Limerick
Day), what they didn't know (the history and tradition of haikus), what they struggled with but could totally do (linking concepts thematically through writing), what they enjoyed (choice,
being silly). I planned activities for Haiku Day not by trying to
cram as much of my own presentation into a fifty-five-minute period as I could, but by what would give my students ample time to
get comfortable with the material, practice, and share.

To this day, it was one of my most fun and memorable days of
teaching.

First, I showed maybe six minutes of an ancient but fantastic
video I found online that explained the origin of haikus and
gave some examples from famous Japanese haiku writers like
Basho and Issa. Instead of having students take notes, I stopped
the video every so often and asked students to explain to their
partners some key pieces of information and occasionally not-
so-key pieces of information. Here are some examples:

"Turn to your partner and tell them one important characteristic of a haiku."

"With your fingers, show me how many syllables the *third* line
of a haiku traditionally has. Please choose appropriate fingers."

"Find someone near you and explain to them what a *kigo*[10] does."

"Raise your hand if you think you can beat me at an impersonation of the narrator of this video."

Then, instead of launching students into their first haiku on their own, we did a few as a class, completing just the final line of a partial haiku, then completing the last two lines of another one, and then composing one on our own. Once we had practiced, I told students they could start working on their own or use one of the haiku "stems"—partially completed haikus—from the video that gave students a complete first line like *A flash of lightning* or the first two lines, like *The kite string broke and/ the loose kite fell fluttering*. I told students that they were free to write silly haikus after they had shown me two traditional haikus linked by theme, and at the end of the period they would have time to share with the class if they wanted.

My Haiku Day classroom was completely different from my Limerick Day classroom. Whatever my students' motivation was—whether it was because they felt successful or they had the opportunity to be silly or because they were feeding off of my own confidence—everyone was busy working, laughing, scrawling their haikus on paper, silently mouthing words while counting syllables on their fingers. My students were asking questions, but they were either small clarifications or probing questions about the material, not questions that revealed any utter confusion about the fundamentals. At the end of the period, I asked if anyone was willing to share their haikus, either a traditional haiku or another one they'd written, and hands flew in the air

---

10 Fun fact: The *kigo* is a word that indicates in which season the haiku is taking place.

like the way hands did in all my teaching dreams. Some haikus
were completely adorable:

> *I see a rainbow*
> *covering the city's sky*
> *with seven colors.*

> *You're so great and tall!*
> *I like your bright, speckled face.*
> *You are a sunflow'r.*

> *Hop out of my way,*
> *Mister Frog, and allow me*
> *My own lily pad.*

Others were a little edgier, taking on some admirable artistic
risks.

> *Look at a chicken.*
> *In the sky up there with a*
> *Big hat on his head.*

> *Hop out of my way,*
> *Mister Frog, and allow me*
> *to eat dirty cats*

We were just about to dismiss for the day when one of my
students, David, spoke up. "Miss! Can I share? I just finished one
more." David's desk partner, who evidently had already read the
poem, stuffed his hands over his mouth and was laughing so
hard that he had turned silent, tears streaming down his face.

"Actually, I changed my mind," David said cautiously.

"Are you sure?" I asked. "Seems like it might be pretty good . . ."

"I'm sure," he said, grinning.

Later that night, I was at my apartment curled up on my couch with a mug of tea, checking over the haikus my students had turned in. I felt like I was soaring. Even my most reluctant writers had written several complete (and correct!) haikus, and one student had even written *Can we do this again?* with a smiley face at the top of his paper. I felt completely different than the way I did after Limerick Day. This was what teaching was supposed to feel like, and I wanted to chase after that feeling.

I was already thinking about how I could make my next lesson feel more like Haiku Day when I got to David's paper. Anxious to read what had made his desk partner laugh so hard, I was disappointed to find that his first several haikus were fairly normal. Somewhat silly, but nothing shocking. Then I flipped his paper over.

> *The tight string broke and*
> *The loose kite fell fluttering*
> *Right into my butt*

We've done Haiku Day every year since.

CHAPTER 8

The Elusive Art of Classroom Management

When I think of what classroom management was like in my early years of teaching, I'm reminded of the same emotions I experience when I spend time with my friend's toddler. The first hour of our visits involves me running after her trying to earn her affection with snacks, questions, and other enticements, and she responds by throwing yogurt-covered fruit snacks at me or shouting, "NO!" as if I couldn't have offended her more with my presence. Eventually I tire and stop trying, and then, for a few fleeting moments when she gives me a pat on my head or hands me a wooden toy cheese wedge, I think I've won her over. My chest swells with pride and I think, *Awww. This is it. This is where you love me.*

Then she grabs a nearby plastic golf club, whacks me over the knees, and laughs.

I don't mean that my students behaved like toddlers, or that the highly nuanced art of classroom management can be reduced to snack offerings (regardless of what Michelle Pfeiffer's character in the film *Dangerous Minds* suggests). I compare them only because in both situations, I had no idea what I was doing and watched as my plans for success went up in flames. In both situations, I was entering someone else's world—their routine, interests, and personality—and trying to relate on my terms but eventually had to learn to do it on theirs. And in both situations, there were no easy answers.

I had one particularly challenging class in which I struggled with classroom management my first year. Even though I wrote down a lot of my stories in journals or in my blog that first year, reflecting on what teaching that class was like is like trying to recall a traumatic head injury—it's all fuzzy and detached, and I only remember little bits and pieces. Memories sometimes come rocketing back to me, seemingly brought on by nothing.

I remember my principal bringing in her boss on what was probably an impromptu visit from him. About thirty seconds into my class I saw her eyes widen as she realized how little control I had over my students, and I watched as she practically frog-marched him out of the room, like, "Nothing to see here!"

I remember a lesson I'd spent hours planning that involved sentence strips, those long, multicolored 3-by-24-inch cardstock strips used for writing practice. After trying and failing for probably twenty minutes to get my students to cooperate, one of them interrupted me and said, "Hey, everyone, put your paper up if you think this class is lame as hell." I looked out on a sea of raised sentence strips, bending slightly like a field of tall, windblown grain. It was kind of pretty, actually.

I remember the Special Ed support teacher, who was assigned to me because of the abundance of students with behavioral challenges in that class period, stopped coming about eight weeks into the school year. She said I appeared to have things under control. I remember thinking, *I would like to die now.*

I remember a precocious student in that class who approached me after class one day at my desk and said, referring to the other students, "Miss, you really need to be tougher on them or they're going to keep walking all over you."

I remember taking two students who were misbehaving into the hall for a serious talk. I was fuming. But suddenly I had an impulse to be vulnerable with these girls instead of scary, so I sighed and said, "Okay. I'm going to be honest. Your behavior is making it really, really tough for me to teach right now. I'm struggling—I'm kind of at the end of my rope here." Just then, one of my students who had bowed her head in what I thought was contrition suddenly snorted, which then caused my other student to throw her head back and cackle. And there, right in front of those students, I burst into tears.

I remember fifteen minutes later sitting alone in the teacher's lounge, trying to sob as quietly as possible. I had been sent there by our school's reading interventionist, who had seen me crying in the hallway and graciously told me she would step in until I had recovered. I fled to the teacher's lounge and wiped at my eyes with my jacket sleeve while exactly three questions marched through my head over and over, like a parade of disappointment:

How can this be happening?
Why do they hate me?
Why is this still so hard?

I'm not the only one who has struggled with classroom management as a new teacher. Every teacher has. Though experiences in classroom management vary from teacher to teacher

and from school to school, I don't know one single educator—
no matter how prestigious their teaching certification program,
no matter how much experience they had with kids, no matter
how glittering their personality, no matter how prepared they
felt—who will say they got to skip over this challenge altogether.[1] A reader once told me that she left her classroom for two
minutes her first year only to come back and discover that her
students had created a wrestling ring with their desks. One of
the best teachers I know told me she went to her administrator
because her entire class of high school juniors would just walk
out of her classroom whenever they felt like it, and her administrators told her *it was her job to have the kind of presence to keep students from walking out.*

Before you throw this book in a fire and vow to stop your pursuit
of teaching altogether, please know that I do not share how
hard classroom management was for me and other teachers to
scare you, nor do I share these stories to bolster some look-at-
how-bad-kids-are-these-days type of propaganda.

I share these stories with you because, as a teacher, you will or
perhaps have already had a day that brings you to your knees—
sometimes because just one day is bad, and sometimes because
the bad days have been on a seemingly unbreakable running
streak—and I want you to know that I have been there. Too
often teachers are afraid to share stories about their bad days,
about times they handled situations poorly, about the nitty-gritty
they had to go through before their teaching looked pretty and
polished. And that's understandable; we're not actually allowed

---

1   If you ever do meet a teacher who claims they didn't struggle with classroom management, know that they are lying or delusional or some kind of robot programmed by the
government to perpetuate damaging myths that teaching is soooo easy.

to be frank about this stuff. When the superintendent of schools, someone with actual power, visits during a faculty meeting and asks how our year is going, it feels weird to say, "Well, I have essentially zero support from my administration and I've discovered I'm terrible at managing a classroom, so every day feels like I'm getting further behind in a race where I'm already in last place, and also my legs are on fire," so instead we say, "Great! It's a privilege to do what we do." As a result, we perpetuate this Perfect Teacher Myth, the one that makes teaching look like an exclusively wonderful job, when really it is wonderful in the way that a mother of newborn triplets might consider her life wonderful. Is teaching an incredible privilege? Absolutely. Is teaching also stressful and exhausting in a way that will occasionally make you think you might not physically survive it? Absolutely. Is teaching an incomprehensibly difficult task without support of some kind? Yes, my friend. Yes, it is.

The absolute toughest part of my rookie years of teaching was the feeling that I was the only teacher who couldn't handle her classroom while everyone else was killing it. So before we go any further in this chapter: If you are struggling in classroom management—whether it's your first year or your tenth or your fortieth—know that you are not alone. Imagine that I'm there with you right now, grabbing you by your shoulders, and saying this to you with wide, serious, slightly maniacal eyes:

YOU ARE NOT ALONE IN FEELING THIS WAY.

Now that we've established that, let's talk about managing a classroom.

Classroom management can look wildly different from school to school and even, depending on who you ask, grade to grade. But one thing to keep in mind is that no matter how supportive or unsupportive your administration is, no matter the particular set of challenges you face in classroom management, and no matter where you are or what age you're teaching, you *do* have a certain amount of power in the decisions you make as a teacher. And you always have agency in choosing how you respond to challenge. It's a good practice to remember the power you do have in a profession that can very often feel powerless.

I've organized my advice for classroom management into a few different areas: mind-set (the way you relate to yourself), attitude (the way you relate outwardly to your students), and the practical (more tangible routines and procedures you can implement no matter what grade you teach).

MIND-SET

You Have to Stop Taking Things Personally as a Classroom Manager

For way too long in my rookie years, I was afraid of what my students thought of me. If I stopped them from running in the hall, would they think I was mean? If I didn't let them choose their own partners for an activity, would I lose my reputation as the Nice Teacher?

One of the most helpful pieces of advice in this area came from Ms. Santiago, a teacher I taught with at my first school and who I mentioned in chapter 4. I met with her one day for advice on what to do about a student of mine who constantly refused to do the warm-up, a two-minute grammar correction exercise. Ms. Santiago encouraged me to be more firm with the student— to talk to him privately about the consequences of not doing the warm-up—and I said something to the effect of, "But I don't want him to think I'm mean." She paused, smiled, and said with all the kindness you could possibly muster toward a teacher who just told you something comically naive, "Listen. At some point, you have to care more about whether your students are safe and learning than what they think of you. Do *you* think it's mean to hold a student accountable for doing the warm-up?" I shook my head no. "Of course it's not! And he won't think so, either. Even if he says you're mean, he will realize that you care enough to make him learn."

When I say Ms. Santiago was telling me to be more firm, she wasn't encouraging me to be nasty or malicious to this student—to this day she has better relationships with her students than any teacher I've ever met. What she meant—advice from her that I've still never forgotten—is that in order to be an effective educator, I had to set aside my ego in the classroom. I had to do what was best for my students. I had to learn that holding students accountable for their safety and their education wouldn't necessarily sacrifice my relationship with them.

Know That Growth Might Look Completely Different Than You Thought It Would

Did you know that the seedling of a blackberry bush can pop up a foot away from where you planted it? And that there are several species of cacti that won't bloom for decades? And that some pine trees actually need a forest fire to burst open their pine cones and release the seeds?

I'm not advocating that you set your classroom on fire. I am, however, encouraging you to be flexible with your vision of what success and growth will look like for your students. Should you have high expectations? Absolutely. But if you have students who are falling short, that doesn't mean they will always be falling short. Some of the most beautiful growth might take years with the combined effort of multiple teachers. It might take something happening that's completely outside of your awareness or control. Growth might be happening right now and you just can't see it. *Don't get discouraged when you don't have an Instagrammable garden by the first report card.*

Be Kind to Yourself

Friend, know this: Classroom management is hard! As you're in the process of learning this incredibly hard thing, give yourself permission to be imperfect and the grace to recover from mistakes—even the big ones. Practice talking to yourself the way you would talk to the person you love most in this world if they were also in the process of learning something hard. If your precious twelve-year-old niece Emma tearfully tells you she's the lamest kid in her seventh-grade class, would you say, "Wow, Emma, I'm so glad you said it first so I didn't have to say it. Get your act together pronto or you will be friendless forever"? Of course not! You would tell Emma how amazing she already is, you would assure her that everyone goes through a rough period in middle school and that it's not always going to feel this way—and you would do everything possible to point out how patently untrue it is that she is in any way lame.

Treat yourself that same way if you're tempted to think disparaging or ugly things about yourself. You're not the worst teacher ever because your classroom management isn't perfect; you're an absolute rock star because you're showing up and you're learning one of the hardest things on this planet.

ATTITUDE
Shoot for a Balance of Firm but Kind

I spent my first two years with the classroom management philosophy that if I just loved my students, they would love me back and learn all the things. (This philosophy had strong roots in my fear of being mean.) The problem with this is that love—real love that is grounded in the respect of other people and the investment in who they're becoming—must also occasionally be tough, because love is insistent and urgent and serious. The magic begins to happen when you find the sweet spot between being firm and kind. *You must be both.*

If you are not firm with your boundaries or procedures, you will communicate that your expectations are low and lose your students' respect. Saying that you expect students to be listening silently while you go over instructions for five minutes but then not intervening when students talk over you sends a very clear message: "I have very low expectations for myself and for you." If you have found yourself feeling like a doormat, you likely need to be more firm about your expectations being met.

If you are not kind to your students or are only kind to certain students, you may get fear-based compliance, but you will have a hard time getting students to connect to your learning in any kind of meaningful way. If your students do what you say but show very little enthusiasm or interest in what's happening in the classroom, you may have nailed the "firm" part but not the "kind" just yet.

Being firm is not the same as being mean, and being nice is not the same as being kind. It's not mean to tell a toddler he can't cross the street by himself. Breaking bad news to a friend may not be nice, but it might be the kind thing to do. It can take a while to find the sweet spot between firm and kind, but always be shooting for firm but kind.

Students Have to Know That You Like Them

I was talking with a teacher friend recently about whether we have to love our students. I do think you have to love all your students—and by "love" I mean you need to have deep respect for who your students are and who they are becoming—but I know that it can be hard to like all of your students all of the time. This can be hard to understand for people who forget that teachers are human beings and not robots. However, this caveat is crucial: I do think you have to behave in a way that makes each of your students think you like *and* love them.

One of the years I had a student teacher, we both observed that my first period was growing increasingly testy, chatty, and all-around difficult. The students wouldn't participate in discussions, and getting classwork from them was like pulling teeth. As a result, my own attitude toward them changed, and I became more sarcastic, harsh, and unpleasant. Once I realized what was happening and the threat it was posing to my students' learning as well as my relationship with them, I told my student teacher what my plan was to turn things around. "I'm going to pretend they're my favorite class."

I'm pretty sure she thought I was insane. We both knew that plenty of my other classes were positive, warm, and full of darlings. How was this a solution, especially since the problem didn't seem like it was my fault? By the way, I decided on this strategy not because I'm any kind of guru, but because I figured "fake it 'til you make it" could work with teaching, too.

Sure enough, once I started slowly rolling out my acting gig and pretended they delighted me—I laughed at their jokes, I made an effort to be enthusiastic, I expressed my gratitude for even the most infinitesimal steps they made in the right direction—we did a 180. They were still my chattiest class by far, but by acting as though I genuinely liked them not just a little bit but a *lot*, they started behaving like the kind of class I liked a lot. And you know what? After a couple of weeks, I didn't even have to pretend.

Stay Calm

I saw a quote on Twitter from Epictetus, a Greek philosopher, recently that I wish I'd read before my first year of teaching: "Any person capable of angering you becomes your master. They can anger you only when you permit yourself to be disturbed by them." The second that you show you're angry or annoyed by raising your voice, you've lost. Even if you think you're winning compliance in the moment by raising your voice or reacting emotionally, you're really losing the respect of that student (and possibly that of others who are witnessing your behavior); I tell you this as someone who's made this mistake with her students countless times. As hard as it can be sometimes when you're pushed to your limit, stay calm in those tough moments.

As Tempting as It Might Be, Don't Argue

I can hear some readers right now—"Don't argue? You've never dealt with *my* students!" *Au contraire*; I have. And I also can't think of a single time that my arguing with a student led to a better relationship with that student. Engaging in an argument shows students that *you* have decided it's okay for them to enter into a battle for power with you. Don't let them enter in the first place!

Instead, with a very soft and gentle voice and with zero sarcasm, use some kind of deescalating statement like, "I understand that," or "I respect you too much to argue." Love and Logic training, which I'll talk more on in the following pages, devotes an entire section on neutralizing student arguments if you want to learn more about this practice.

PRACTICAL
Next to Relationships, Procedures Are Everything

So, so, so much of classroom management comes down to the procedures you implement and whether you enforce them. For instance, a few years ago a teacher asked me to observe a class she was having trouble managing. I noticed the chaos started with the way students entered the classroom—running, yelling, throwing paper, all of which disturbed the students who were trying to work on the warm-up. I asked the teacher teaching the class whether she had a policy for how students should enter the classroom, and she said, "Oh, yes—they know they're supposed to come in and get started." But the thing is, if you're frustrated with a certain behavior in class, one of three things is happening:

1. The students haven't been told the procedure for how to behave,
2. They haven't practiced the procedure enough, or
3. The procedure hasn't been enforced consistently.

Notice what specific behaviors are bothering you in your classroom, implement a procedure to curb it, and stick to it.

Are students interrupting direct instruction or having trouble raising their hands? Implement a procedure that when you're talking to the whole class, students are silent, paying attention, and raising their hand if they have a question. For practice, tell students, "I'm about to start whole-group instruction. Someone remind me of our procedure." Practice this any time you're talking to the whole class, and when someone forgets, say, "Oh, I see you forgot our procedure. That's okay. What's the procedure when I'm talking to the class?"

Are students taking way too long to transition between activities? Start a procedure that, during a transition, students are on task, quiet, and complete the transition before a timer goes off. For practice, any time you need to move on to a new activity, say, "We're going to transition to journaling now. You have two minutes to get your journal, open to a new page, and write your heading. Someone remind me of our procedure during transitions." Practice this during every transition until students can't get it wrong.

You can use this process for anything in your classroom that becomes a struggle or is wasting the learning time of your students. What you're willing to put up with may be different from another teacher down the hall. For instance, when a student sharpens their pencil while I'm talking to the class, it makes me want to curl up on the floor and die, come back as a ghost, and spend eternity haunting the area next to the pencil sharpener, grabbing the forearms of future offenders with my ice-cold spectral fingers. The math teacher next door to me, Linda, isn't phased at all by mid-lecture pencil sharpening but has trouble reading assignments when students turn them in on overly crinkled paper, which is something I certainly don't endorse but have never been bothered by as a teacher. Rather than complain about these things two thousand times per school year, both Linda and I have classroom procedures we've created and review at the beginning of the year to address them and prevent them from happening. Don't panic if the teacher next door has a procedure that you don't or vice versa; as long as neither of you is sacrificing significant instructional time or the relationships with your students, you do you.

Use Visual Tools to Make Instructions and Expectations Clear

I'm a big believer that chaos ensues when students are confused (BRB—I'm off to trademark that rhyming expression).

Think about it for a second, though: *Chaos ensues when students are confused.* This totally happens with adults, too. Have you ever been at a football game when there's a pause in the game and no one can figure out why? Or what about when there's a traffic jam on a one-lane road, but you can't see the blockage from your vantage point? What happens? People start getting out of cars. People start raising their voices. People get on their phones—to pass the time or complain or rage-tweet.

The same thing happens in the classroom. If your instructions or expectations are unclear or inaccessible, you can count on students to start getting antsy, distracted, or off task. Students need to know what they should be doing, what the expectations are for completing their assignment, where they can get their materials, and what they should do when they're done. (Also note: Just because *you* think your instructions are clear doesn't necessarily mean they are).☺

One big way to cut down on confusion if your students are of reading age is to make sure you have posted legible instructions/expectations for each day or even for each activity on the board. My practice of doing this dramatically cut down on student confusion in my classroom. Students who actually wanted to be on task were way less frustrated about the expectations, and students who didn't want to be on task couldn't say they didn't know what they were supposed to be doing. Bonus: I was able to focus on actually teaching and helping my students with the content instead of answering and re-answering questions about the assignment 1,592 times.

Learn the Love and Logic Philosophy

Love and Logic is a parenting and teaching philosophy that makes adults less bonkers and their relationships with kids more enjoyable. At least that's my take. On their website, it says they "provide practical tools and techniques that help adults achieve respectful, healthy relationships with their children."

The *Love, Teach* rundown of Love and Logic is this: L&L is a series of simple (like, so simple you might be dubious) strategies to help you communicate to your students that you notice them, are invested in them, and that they have a voice in the decisions that happen involving them in the classroom.

You know I wouldn't recommend anything that wasn't effective in a wide range of schools, and this training has my official endorsement. But you should know that like any skill or approach, teaching with love and logic takes practice and a long-game willingness to learn. The only people I've seen flat out reject the philosophy are people who went into training already believing that their way was better, or who tried it for a few days and were angry that their classroom didn't get an instant Hollywood transformation.

Create a Support Network

It is super important to build the right kind of community as a teacher. Identify three very important people to be in your classroom management support group:

- One new teacher, even if you have to find them online, who will laugh with you about your struggles in classroom management. I know I've seen so many mini support groups pop up in the comments sections of my blog posts or Facebook statuses, which is one of the many reasons I'm so grateful for the *Love, Teach* community.
- One experienced teacher who is willing to observe your classroom every once in a while and give you kind but

honest feedback. If you're not sure who to ask, contact an administrator at your school or someone at the district level. Often there are entire teams of people designated to help new teachers manage their classrooms. Sometimes they're just waiting for teachers to reach out!

- One cheerleader who is available to listen when things get tough, who can guide you to things that make you happy and redirect you toward self-care when necessary. This person can be a friend, a significant other, a therapist, or a religious or spiritual leader. Just be aware of how much you're "unloading" on this other person (unless they are a professional). Teaching is a *lot*, whether you're the one experiencing it or the person listening to all of the stories about it.

CHAPTER 9

Ah, Parents.

As a new teacher, I was terrified of my students' parents. For one thing, I was afraid of how mad they would be once they found out that I was completely underqualified to be in charge of their children's brains. From other teachers I knew, I also had heard a lot of horror stories about the way parents can behave. Friends told me about condescending e-mails they'd received, times they'd gotten yelled at in parent-teacher conferences, and I even heard stories about some parents who had threatened to file lawsuits. I was sure the same thing would happen to me, and the thought of this added a nervous, almost frantic edge to my interactions with parents. One of my first voicemails to a parent sounded very close to this: "Oh, yeah, hi, this is Raul, and I'm calling about Ms. Treleaven. Oh, nope. Hahaha. I'm Ms. Treleaven. Raul is . . . my student. Well, hopefully we can talk about his behavior soon. If you could call me back when you get a chance, my number is . . . You know what, I actually don't know my phone number here yet. Have a great . . . night. Bye-bye."

Luckily, in my experience, the horror stories weren't true by a long shot. I could talk about the parents who have made demands so unreasonable they border on comical, or the 1,500-word e-mail diatribe sent my way for not accepting a late assignment after grades went in, even though I'd entered the grade as a sixty to avoid doing too much damage to the student's average. But the truth is, for the most part, no matter what school I've taught in, from schools where most of the kids were on free or reduced lunch programs to a school with children from one of the state's wealthiest zip codes, almost all the parents I've known have been gracious, reasonable, kind people who want the best for their child and value me as a professional. For every parent who has made me miserable, I can tell you stories of five parents who have come through for me in the ninth inning, parents with psychic powers who have managed to send an iced coffee or an old butter container filled with *caldo de pollo* at exactly the time I needed it the most, parents who have written me the world's sweetest notes, and parents who have put an enormous amount of trust in me and my decisions and made my job infinitely easier. Though I still empathize with my brand-new teacher self, it turns out I had very little need to be nervous of my students' parents.

It's important to know that parents today do have a bigger role in the classroom than ever before. This is not always a bad thing—I'm happy for parents and community members to play more active roles in schools. Removing a bit of the wall, so to speak, between school and home has made parents feel more a part of their children's learning, and I think it's better for everyone in the long run to be a team rather than for the teacher to wield all the power in a veil of secrecy.

I do, however, believe that in moving away from teachers having all the power, we've gone a little too far in the opposite direction and it can be easy for teachers to feel powerless. Advances in technology have given parents near-instant access to teachers via e-mail, they can opt to receive instant notifications seconds after a grade is posted in the gradebook, and they can even get texts about teachers from their child's point of view moments after they are wronged. Experts have observed that we are in an age of overparenting—parents feel obligated to intervene and shield their children from failure rather than prepare their children to wrestle with problems on their own. Meanwhile, educational policies have put more and more work, strain, and accountability on teachers and their classes' test scores, leaving students with less responsibility for their learning.

I don't know how to swing the pendulum to a place where power is shared, where parents and teachers are mutually respectful of each other, and where the teaching profession is so well supported that it attracts the most qualified, elite force of educators the world has ever seen.

However, I do know how to protect yourself and build relationships with *your* group of parents in a world that's not quite perfect yet.

First, there's a strong chance you may already have some assumptions about parents, whether or not you've begun teaching yet. Let's go over some of the myths, truths, and half-truths about parents and their role in the classroom.

PARENTS IN TITLE I SCHOOLS DON'T CARE. *MYTH.*

Teachers in Title I schools often face frustrating situations involving parents. It's not uncommon to experience things like:

- A parent missing a parent-teacher conference
- Child behavior problems that don't improve despite parent contact
- Repeated instances of a child not turning in homework or classwork despite parent contact

For teachers, these kinds of situations stir up emotions. We feel protective over the kids we love and angry that their circumstances aren't improving, and we sometimes jump to conclusions about what must be happening at home. We assume the parent must be too lazy to enforce any kind of real discipline or an after-school homework routine at the kitchen table. We assume that a parent who misses a parent-teacher conference doesn't care about their child: Why else would they be a no-show?

But it's important to remember that we don't see what's happening behind the scenes. We don't see the interaction in which the parent asks her son every day, "Did you do your homework?" and then is told he already did it or he doesn't have any. We don't see a student's younger sibling with special needs, who requires constant supervision, and whose condition isn't covered under their insurance. We don't see the dad who wants to be involved but who can't risk losing his job to come to a school meeting at 11:00 a.m. We don't see that the parent has taken away every privilege except for video games because it keeps her son where she can see him.

We're not aware of the experiences these parents may have had in the past with businesses and institutions—shop owners eyeing them carefully as they follow them around a store, a shaming experience with a poorly trained police officer, a post office worker rolling his eyes when he realizes he has to go get a Spanish-speaking coworker. Parents with children at Title I schools may have already had their parenting questioned by the school—a kindergarten teacher calling to find out why the reading log wasn't filled out when it's such an easy assignment, a second-grade teacher pressuring to know if there are consequences at home for bad behavior. It's no wonder that some of these parents avoid schools altogether—they are often conditioned to feel powerless in their interactions with the school, or they are accused of not doing enough.

When you look at poor children through the distorted lens of wealth, you'll make harmful assumptions about people and values. If a super-wealthy billionaire visited my home, they might say I don't value my safety because I'm not driving a luxury car with a five-star safety rating, or that my dog is suffering because he doesn't get weekly acupuncture. It's just as insulting to assume that parents don't care because they aren't hiring nannies or tutors or other solutions that wealthier people have available to them.

Now, are *all* parents in Title I schools doing their best to be involved and advocate for their child and support learning at home? No, and teachers in Title I schools are no strangers to having to report abuse or neglect. But we can't perpetuate a myth that lets us dismiss an entire population. It's harmful to our own relationships with these parents, our students, and just other humans in general.

ALL PARENTS IN WEALTHY SCHOOLS ARE OBSESSIVE HELICOPTER PARENTS. *MYTH.*

Much like the myth that parents in Title I schools don't care, the myth about helicopter parents in wealthy schools has little truth to it. Are there obsessive, overprotective, anxiety-fueled parents who e-mail the teacher the second grades go in, demanding that you scan them the worksheet so they can evaluate it themselves? Yes. But are most of the parents I've met kind, reasonable people who understand that their children are imperfect, trust my professional judgment, and understand that mistakes are a part of growth and not indicative of a life of failure? Yes. And have I seen plenty of overprotective, anxiety-fueled parents cool their jets as the school year goes on to reveal that they are perfectly normal and fair people who were simply behaving unreasonably? Also yes.

From my interviews with longtime veteran teachers in a range of schools across the country, it's clear that there's a growing mistrust of teachers among parents. I'd argue that the two big factors contributing to this are: educational policies that put too much of the responsibility for our broken system on teachers, as well as the myth that getting into a certain college is requisite for a child's success and personal happiness. I don't know that parents have changed so much—it seems that the entire country has taken the lead from our government to treat teachers like untrustworthy, corner-cutting contractors who need constant monitoring instead of highly qualified, trained professionals.

That's depressing news, I know. But the good news is that there are a lot of relatively easy things you can do to convince parents who have a tendency to be helicopter-y that you have their child's best interest in mind and that, believe it or not, you are indeed a highly qualified, trained professional (we'll discuss them at the end of this chapter). You won't win them all, but you'll keep yourself way more sane and your workload way more manageable. Which conveniently leads me to the next myth I must debunk:

I'M A BAD TEACHER IF I'M STRUGGLING WITH PARENTS. *MYTH.*

If you gathered all fifty Teachers of the Year from each state in one room and asked them how many of them have been frustrated by a parent this school year, I have very little doubt that all fifty would raise their hands. It doesn't matter how talented, how prepared, how communicative, how professional, how caring you are—you will always have some parent who thinks you're not doing enough or that you're not doing things the right way.

If you're reading this and thinking, *Yeah, but I'll be different,* trust me—it's better to come to terms with this now than to exhaust yourself by trying and failing to be the perfect teacher. Once, on the same day, I got e-mails from two different parents, one saying I give too much homework and one saying I'm underpreparing my students because I don't give enough. In that same school year, I was told by two different parents that I was both teaching too much creative writing and that I wasn't giving students enough opportunities to write creatively.

As a teacher, you have to accept—and I would even encourage you to laugh about—the fact that you will not please everyone. *There's no such thing as the perfect teacher.*

I HAVE NO CONTROL OVER THE WAY PARENTS FEEL ABOUT ME. *HALF-TRUTH.*

Like many situations you will face in the teaching world, balance is the key. From what I've observed, the teachers who tend to struggle the most with parents are the ones who haven't found balance between working with parents and standing up for themselves. The teachers who bend to parents' every whim are miserable because they have no agency in their own classroom. On the other hand, the teachers who refuse to budge on any parent request are miserable because parents feel *they* have no agency and are caught in a negative feedback loop trying to assert their power. The healthiest teachers I know are the ones who have found a place in the middle. They listen to parents (even the frustrating ones), work together with them in a reasonable way, and stand their ground when necessary because of the relationships they've worked to put in place.

Even though none of us can be the perfect teacher, there *are* things you can do to increase the transparency of your teaching and to help communicate that you, in fact, are a trained profes-sional and that you have their child's best interests at heart. True, you can't control how parents feel, but you do control some of the information they receive from you that informs their opinions.

- **First impressions are everything.** Parents want to know that their children have a teacher who is qualified, but they also want to know that the teacher likes their child. I would strongly recommend putting in the time and energy—even though it's a lot, trust me from experience—to reach out to each parent in the first few weeks with something positive to say, whether it's a Post-it note, a one-line e-mail, something that lets them know you're glad their child is in your class. This doesn't just have to be a thing for elementary kids, either—I joke with my secondary students that my little note written on apple stationery is a fantastic bargaining chip for the next time they petition their parents for a treat or reward.

- **Set communication boundaries with parents.** Set the tone early on that you are happy to communicate with them but that it needs to be on your terms. Whether it's through a weekly newsletter or a website or a blog that you update, let parents know right away how they can stay in the loop with what's going on in your classroom. This is not just good for parents to know, but it is important to document in case it's needed later (i.e., "But we had no idea science fair was this week."). Also, with the increasingly hyperconnected world we live in, it's important to set boundaries with your use of e-mail. Personally, I wouldn't recommend responding to any parent e-mail outside of school hours unless it's a time-sensitive emergency—it's crucial for your self-care to separate home and work. If you find that you can't send a quick reply or if the parent has sent you an inappropriately long or rude e-mail, respond with something like, "Thank you so much for your e-mail. I definitely want to give this topic the time and attention it deserves. Could we set up a meeting sometime this week to discuss it?"

- **Use empowering language and always give parents the benefit of the doubt first.** Instead of "Well, do you discipline Johnny when he does something wrong?" show them you believe in their parenting and say something like, "What kind of consequences are effective with Johnny at home? I'm curious if there's something you can share that works with him." If they say, "We actually don't believe in consequences, boundaries, or the word 'no,'" then you can frown.

- **Document every interaction with parents.** I have a spreadsheet I use with columns for the date, time, student, parent, method of contact (e-mail, phone, in-person conference), and notes. I write down what was discussed, what was decided, what the tone of the interaction was like, everything. I can't tell you how many times this has saved me from cries of "But we were never notified!" or "Well, Ms. Treleaven called once, but that was weeks ago" or "I never agreed to *that*." I've used my parent contact log multiple times to identify patterns in student behavior or to help parents connect certain behaviors to certain times—examples include switching medications, a traumatic event, and staying up late every night for two weeks to watch the World Series. Another good thing to do is to have another teacher scribe notes for you if you're on the phone (put the call on speaker mode) or meeting in person. That way, you can give your full attention to the parent, while also maintaining a record of what you talked about (just be sure to give the parent a heads-up if you're having someone scribe on the phone—assure them that they are there to make sure you hold yourself accountable for any changes or decisions you agree on). Also, parents are way less likely to behave badly if there's a second party there, listening to and writing down what they're saying.

- **Be transparent.** The more your students' parents know about what's happening in the classroom, the better. I cut down on a ton of confusion with parents and students the year that I started posting an online calendar with homework assignments, copies of notes, test and project due dates, and what we'd done in class. Something that takes three minutes to do each week saved me hours of e-mails and parent conferences and tons of stress. It also cut down on the following student utterances that, at one time, threatened to drive me insane:

  ~ "I didn't know when the project was due/there would be a quiz."
  ~ "I couldn't do my homework because I didn't have the notes."
  ~ "What did I miss yesterday when I was absent?"

....

Six Pro Tips for Scary Parent Conferences

If you have an upcoming conference with parents who may have an antagonistic bent (or if you're not yet confident in your conference abilities), here are some tips to have the healthiest, most productive interaction possible.

1. Don't be alone. Bring a fellow teacher or an administrator you trust to take notes during the meeting, and be absolutely sure you introduce this person to the parent and the reason for them being there. "This is my colleague, Ms. Watson—is it okay if she stays with us to type up notes today? That way she can e-mail us both at the end with a record of what we discussed and what decisions might be made." Note: This is a good practice for all conferences!

2. Bring documentation. The more facts and data you can gather ahead of time, the better. You may not end up needing it, but it can be really helpful to support your points with evidence. Sometimes, if the discussion hinges on academic work, I include (with the name redacted) a sample of another student's work to show a parent what mastery looks like and use it to discuss how to get their child to that point.

3. Start out on the right foot. Sometimes a scared parent will come to a meeting with set beliefs—the teacher "has it out" for their child, their student is incapable of success, etc. Start the meeting with something like, "It's always important for me to start parent conferences with a shared purpose. I really enjoy having Keith in my class. I would love for him to feel successful in algebra, and I want us to leave today with a sense of how to make that happen. I know a lot happens that I don't see, so first I'd love to hear about what's been going on from your perspective." You're establishing 1) a shared purpose; 2) that you're not out to get their child; and 3) that you're here to listen and that their voice matters.

4. Don't react to bad behavior. Remember, any parent behaving badly is coming from a place of genuine fear for their child.

Don't give in if they call you names, make false accusations, or raise their voice. However, you absolutely should not tolerate abuse from parents. If their behavior doesn't improve, calmly suggest that you're worried you might not reach a place of mutual understanding today, and that it may be better to continue the discussion another time (that is, when an administrator is present who can put an end to their bad behavior).

5. Don't agree to anything you're not 100 percent sure is the right move. I always felt a lot of pressure as a new teacher to agree to whatever the parent wanted, even if it was ridiculous. There's nothing wrong with saying, "I'll need to check the grading guidelines first before I can confirm that, but I'll get back to you," or "Let me check with our department chair first to run that by her—we may have a departmental procedure for that kind of thing."

6. Follow up afterward. Follow up immediately with an e-mail including the notes from whoever was typing for you, and re-establish that you're so grateful for the parent's time and for coming in today. Explain when the next follow-up will be (next day? three days? one week?) to ensure that their child is on the path to success.

· ·

Some teachers might say that putting the homework assignments online is "cheating" somehow, that it undermines students learning organizational habits involved in writing assignments down in a planner, or that it allows parents to be able to do the homework for them. To that I say:

1. Students still have to sit down, check the assignment, and do the work.
2. Even if parents are doing the homework for them—which is 10 percent of their grade—the classwork, quizzes, and tests students will take are a much bigger percentage.
3. I never learned how to use a paper-and-pencil planner. I'm doing just fine. In fact, *I look up almost everything online.*

• Make instructions for home projects crystal clear. Transparency and setting a positive tone can work wonders, but another thing to be in the habit of is working hard to make sure there is unshakable clarity on your assignments— especially projects. Don't ask yourself, *Are these instructions and expectations clear to me?* Ask yourself, *Could these instructions and expectations possibly be misconstrued by a parent or child?* A common mistake made by new teachers is to create assignments with crazy long or wordy instructions and complex assignments without a rubric (or with a vague rubric).

• Remember that any "bad" behavior from parents comes from a place of fear. This is one of the best pieces of advice I've ever received. Parents who have resorted to hostility or rage are deeply, painfully afraid for their child. Sometimes this fear is justified. Other times, it can be hard to remember that the parent is scared and vulnerable, like when a mom says on the phone that your English undergraduate degree must have been a sham. But thinking about this piece of advice reminded me that the parent's anger had nothing to do with where I went to college, or even me—it had everything to do with her worry that her son was somehow behind or at risk of not getting the kind of future that would make him happy.[2] And I can empathize with that.

- View parents as your allies. Even if they're behaving as your adversary, consider that this is just the part of the story before they become your ally. You know the people who talk about how the feelings you project into the universe become reality? Well, in this case, I think those people are right. If you go into teaching convinced that all parents will be horrible and that your entire career you will be fending them off with a stick, you'll probably make the first parent to e-mail you with a question out to be a malicious villain, or you'll assume the first parent to request a conference is attacking your professional capabilities. Alternatively, if you take the point of view that parents are your allies, you might look at parent questions as just that—questions—or meetings as opportunities for teamwork to arrive at a point of mutual understanding and growth.

- Advocate for your own professionalism and passion for the subject. As a new teacher, it can feel very daunting to be in a role assuring people who are likely older than you that you know what you're doing and that their child's brain is in capable hands. And it's true that you will have days when you doubt your effectiveness. *But remember that you wouldn't be teaching if you didn't believe that you were a capable teacher.* In your back-to-school letter or on parent night, don't be afraid to talk about your qualifications, experience working with kids, or the professional training you've had. Talk about

---

2 Note: I didn't ask for my supervisor to intervene in this instance, but you should always feel free to ask an administrator for support if you feel like a parent is being insulting or threatening.

what made you fall in love with math or teaching kindergarten and what fuels that passion. Parents want to know that you know what you're doing and that you *care* about what you're doing.

- Listen. Starting conferences or phone calls by listening is a good way to disarm potential tension.

  - "I want to make sure that your concerns are put to ease today. Why don't we start by you telling me a little of what you hope to get out of today's meeting."
  - "I'm so glad you could make it here today. I love to start conferences by hearing about your child. Tell me about Emilia."
  - "I want to make sure you feel heard. Tell me about your perspective."
  - "I'd love to know ways I can help you."

Don't be afraid if you start off the year with a parent (or several) who don't seem to be 100 percent in your corner. Maybe you wish they were able to have a more involved role in their child's education, or maybe you wish they were way *less* involved. I know what both of those feelings are like. I hope that as a country we're moving in a direction where all parents feel welcome in schools, trust teachers as a default, and approach misunderstandings from a place of mutual respect. But until then, be transparent. Be communicative. And when you hear an adult voice say, "Ms. Treleaven!" in a Mexican restaurant after your second large margarita, just smile and nod until the interaction is over.

CHAPTER 10

Administration

If you're reading the title of this chapter and thinking to yourself, *I can skip this chapter—I've never had a problem with authority,* you're exactly the type of person who needs this section most. I'm willing to bet that many of you, like me, have probably lived your life in a way that is either pleasing to authority or keeps you off their radar. And maybe you've never had a reason to challenge the person in charge—you've always had reasonably competent teachers, coaches, and bosses. Or if you've had a conflict, you've been able to stand up for yourself in a thoughtfully worded, diplomatic way that actually resulted in the change or solution you wanted. I'm willing to bet that working hard and being kind has, so far, always been pretty good to you when it comes to dealing with authority figures.

The teaching world can be a little different.

Let me give you a sense of the range of administrative personality types I've worked with in my time as a teacher at several different schools.

I've worked for an administrator who held a custodian as she cried, upset that it would be her first Thanksgiving without her father.

I've worked for an administrator who asked me and another teacher to write her admissions essays for an Ivy League principal's institute.

I've worked for an administrator who watched—and taught— all my classes for an entire day so I could go to a doctor's appointment that he knew mattered and would be very hard to reschedule.

I've worked for an administrator who pushed a student into the wall using the handle of his rolling backpack, then said, "I didn't touch you. My hands never touched you." All of this in front of me and another teacher.

I've worked with an administrator who had enough faith in me to let me implement a structured silent reading program and went to bat for me when my own administration was critical of the program.

I've worked with an administrator who wrote an e-mail that got intercepted by another faculty member[1] in which she referred to her own history department as "a bunch of skinny white bitches."

I've worked under an administration that kept me from burning out; that showed me there are heroes in educational leadership who are not only brilliant at what they do but care deeply about what they do.

I've worked under an administration that, even the thought of meeting with them, gave me regular panic attacks on Sunday afternoons for months.

Are there heroes working in school administration? Absolutely.

---

1 This apparently was not enough to remove her from consideration for multiple promotions, by the way.

Are there also garbage people leading schools where children are being educated?[2] Unfortunately, yes.

I remember the role-playing scenarios in my teaching books when I was taking education classes, little snippets of possible difficult situations teachers might encounter with administration. Things like:

In a recent evaluation, your appraiser criticized the use of a teaching strategy you know to be effective. How do you approach a conversation with her?

You lead a popular grade-level book club for students, but your principal says there's no money for your club in next year's budget. How do you handle this?

These are laughable to me now. The role-play scenarios should have been more like this:

One of your eighth-grade students, James, tells you he got in-school suspension for something that allegedly happened in your class that you have no recollection of. You ask your assistant principal, Mr. West, about the situation and he responds, "Wow. If I were you, I wouldn't question the authority of the person who I know is doing my teaching evaluations. But then again, I'm pretty smart." You know you should tell someone, but your principal has made a point of telling the faculty that she always has her assistant principals' backs. What do you do when you suspect a student has been wronged, but you've been threatened into silence?

The good news is that you probably won't encounter situations that dramatic. These are the kind of stories I only share when I find myself talking to a teacher who may need a little perspective on their situation with an administrator (e.g., "Mr.

---

2   I try to avoid negative labels like these, but people who threaten the emotional or physical safety of kids are, to me, made of garbage.

Richards is the worst administrator ever for making us come to meetings on time!"), since they are not the kind of stories that illustrate commonplace administrator misbehavior. I should also add that in my time as a teacher, most of the administrators I've worked with have either been wonderful or at least competent.

But unfortunately, I am confident that you will certainly encounter at least one less-than-stellar administrator in your teaching career. Some of these are people who are on their way to being good leaders but still learning. Some of these administrators started out as teachers who, understandably, realized they couldn't support a family on a paltry teacher salary, and who decided to go into administration for more money even though they were uninterested in or not well suited for the job. Some are weak leaders because they are afraid of conflict; some are weak because they drum up conflict at every opportunity.

If you remain a teacher for long, you will encounter these bad apples. You may know right away, or it may take a few months or years. They may brandish their ineffectiveness out in the open, or their bad behavior may be more subtle and passive-aggressive. But you need to be able to navigate these types of administrators, as well as know how to protect yourself and your job.

First, let's talk about the typical administrative hierarchy in a school, since being aware of the setup of power is important in understanding yours and others' roles in the workplace. At the top of the command in a school is a principal or director with one or several assistant principals beneath them. While the principal or head director is ultimately "in charge," you will probably have more interaction and visibility with the second tier of leadership, made up of the assistant principals (APs, sometimes called deputy principals), deans, or people with other administrative titles. The leaders in this second tier of power can have a variety of responsibilities. Some are tasked with organizing the beast of standardized testing, some are the go-to contact for maintenance issues, from getting the track repaired to dealing with a school-wide power outage. But almost all APs are also tasked with appraising a group of teachers, which is where a big part of your connection with administration comes in. The administrator charged with being your appraiser will be in your classroom several times throughout the year to conduct formal and informal observations of your teaching, provide you with feedback of what's working and what needs improvement, and follow up on what changes have taken place (before school even starts you should be informed about what appraisers are looking for). Some schools have appraisers schedule observations with teachers; others conduct random observations. Typically, schools will try to assign appraisers based on the appraiser's teaching experience—a former English teacher might appraise the humanities department, or a former physics teacher might appraise the science department. But an appraiser's experience and your subject area might not always match up.

You can imagine, then, the types of situations—positive and negative—that can arise with this kind of power arrangement. An assistant principal with two years of teaching music at an elementary school could be appraising a twenty-year veteran calculus teacher. (It's important to note that this difference in experience could be unhelpful or illuminating!) An appraiser could choose a Wednesday in October for a teacher's formal forty-five-minute observation, or "randomly" choose two o'clock on the Friday before winter break, when hardly any teachers in their right mind are teaching new or vital content and the children are peak-level rambunctious. Any school leader should be com-

mitted to helping teachers improve and making their jobs easier (and many of them are), but every job has its bad apples.

Clearly, administrators have the potential to affect a lot that
goes on in a school, from what's happening in a particular classroom to the overall culture. It's important to establish positive
relationships with administration early to make your job (and
theirs) easier.

I've divided my advice in this chapter into two different
sections. The first is about creating and preserving positive
relationships with administration, because it's completely possible. The second section is the advice I really needed as a new
teacher, regarding what to do when you've been doing everything right but find yourself in a toxic situation: how to protect
yourself, possibly alleviate the situation, or know when to get out.

CREATING AND MAINTAINING POSITIVE
RELATIONSHIPS WITH ADMINISTRATION

Here are some guidelines I suggest for laying the groundwork
for a positive relationship with administrators based on mutual
trust and respect:

When the stakes are low, go with the flow. As a teacher, you are
going to be asked to do things that are inconvenient or
that you don't agree with. But when the stakes are
low—tasks that don't compromise your teaching or your
relationship with your students—you will make your
administration's jobs so much easier by doing what you're
asked. Yes, your principal might send a lot of long e-mails.
But because reading e-mails doesn't compromise your
teaching or your relationship with your students, it's not
something worth making a fuss over or taking a stance that
you're not going to read them. If your administration asks

teachers to wear pink for Spirit Week, do it. You are shooting for Team Player, not Team Curmudgeon.

Keep your cards close to your vest when talking to peers. Regardless of how you feel about various administrators, avoid sounding off to anyone for a while, especially at a new school. Gossip travels fast and can be twisted very easily. Also, it's worth knowing that some people may try to bait you for information to report back directly to your administrators. I know, because a principal asked me to find out how the English department felt about a certain AP and report back. I didn't, because that seemed immature and unprofessional to me—but it's an additional reason to lay low with negative opinions.

Remember that administrators are on your team. It can be easy to separate yourself from administration with an "us vs. them" mentality. But if administrators are doing their jobs well, you should all be on the same team, working together to make sure kids learn at the highest levels. While it's good to maintain professional boundaries with administration, remember that they're people, too. Don't be afraid to ask about the picture of their kids on their desk, their interests, their "World's Best Boss" mug that you can tell is a nod to *The Office*. Also, try to extend special grace to administrators who are new parents in their first couple of years as an administrator, or in other life situations that might make it tougher to be the perfect leader.

Be the first one to tell them bad news. Administrators don't like to be surprised with negative information, so if there's an opportunity for you to give them a heads-up in time for an intervention, take it. If you're really struggling with classroom management, rather than wait for administrators to discover this themselves in an observation, go to them first and ask if they can connect you with district resources or professional development opportunities. If you make a serious mistake in the classroom, like, I don't know, asking a student to move a lamp for you and the lamp shatters and cuts up a student's hand, rather than wait for a parent to call, tell your administrator, "Hey, I really messed up. I want to be transparent and make sure you know as soon as possible. What should my next course of action be?"

Welcome and embrace critical feedback. Throughout your career as a teacher but especially in your rookie years, you are not going to know everything. You will need to get very comfortable very fast with accepting criticism. When an administrator identifies an area of weakness for you to work on, be grateful—this is how you improve! Look at the difference between the responses of a teacher who is grateful for critical feedback and a teacher who has her defenses up big-time:

> Assistant Principal: In your lesson, I noticed that several times when you asked questions, you answered them almost immediately instead of giving students wait time. That might be an area to work on in the future—extending your wait time.

> Defensive Teacher: Well, I never learned about wait time in my education courses, so I'm not sure how I was supposed to know to do that. But okay.

> Grateful Teacher: Oh, okay—that's something I hadn't considered before. Thanks for pointing that

out. I'm not familiar with wait time—is it typically a few seconds, or several minutes?

WHAT TO DO WHEN YOU'RE STRUGGLING WITH YOUR ADMINISTRATION

Okay. This is what I needed in my new-teacher books.

I want to first start by saying something that might be difficult to hear: It's critical you recognize the difference between whether you actually have a bad administrator . . . or simply have a bad attitude. The following section is *not* for the teachers who go against the grain at every available opportunity, use gossip as their primary means of communication, and thrive by creating drama and bad-mouthing their boss.

This is for the teachers who work hard to develop their professional skills at every opportunity, who are kind in their interactions, who hold integrity as a top value, and still aren't getting the kind of support they need from their administration—either because their leaders are indifferent, ineffective, or even creating or contributing to a hostile workspace.

My advice for teachers in the latter situation is this:

Document, document, document. This is a good habit to have as a teacher, even if you're not struggling, but definitely keep a record of any maltreatment you have in your interactions with administration. This can be helpful both in protecting yourself and in building a case should the need arise. I still have a whole document of dates and descriptions of unethical and unprofessional behavior from an AP at one of my former schools. Though I didn't end up filing a formal complaint (largely because I felt there weren't the kinds of structures in place for me to do so without being targeted), creating that document was good practice for knowing how to safeguard myself in future scenarios.

And it was empowering during a time when I felt mostly helpless and voiceless. If you do end up taking complaints to HR or some other representative who can help you, this information will be invaluable.

Go through my three-step process before picking a battle with administration. Okay. Here's where I diverge pretty hard from standard teaching books.

Most books will say that if you disagree with a policy implemented by administration, you should always make an appointment with an administrator and calmly discuss your concerns until you reach a compromise.

That works great.

. . . if your administrators are reasonable, intelligent, openminded people who can accept critical feedback without equating it with a personal attack, or immediately planning retaliation. (They're plenty out there, but not everywhere.)

If your administrators are *not* these kind of people, this doesn't mean you have to be a complete doormat until you can get out of that school. It just means that you may have to be strategic about which issues you choose to dispute. Before you decide to confront your administration, go through these three steps:

1. Think about what's at stake. If the issue doesn't affect your students' health or safety, devalue their or your humanity, compromise their ability to learn, or negatively impact your ability to teach or your work environment—is it a battle worth fighting?
2. List all your options and their consequences. Be creative and think of all the possible consequences, positive and negative, even if they seem unlikely. Would your administration be grateful for your feedback, or would

there be potential retaliation? What might retaliation look like given the people involved? Could you be asked to lead a committee solving this problem? Could there be a lawsuit? Thinking through all the possible consequences will help you in making an informed decision instead of a purely reactive one.

3. Make a decision based on your needs, your students' needs, and the consequences you are willing to accept. The consequences you are willing to accept will likely change with experience and under different leaders. Now that I've been teaching for close to a decade and I am under an administration I trust, I feel comfortable enough to be honest if high-stakes issues were to come up that I strongly oppose. But in past years, I would often decide at this step not to confront administration. Here's where I give you advice that is not entirely professional: Sometimes in the world of education it's better to ask for forgiveness than permission, and *sometimes the semblance of compliance is better than actual compliance.*

In a system that often works against teachers and students, sometimes you have to rebel a little bit to get anything done.

If you decide to confront administration, an attitude of curiosity is better than an attitude of hostility. Let's say your principal made a decision about a new tardy policy you think is bonkers. Now, when a student is tardy, the teacher sends the student back to a tardy desk (manned by a teacher on their conference period) to get a tardy slip, adding nearly five minutes of missed class for an already tardy student and creating additional work for teachers. After going through the three-step decision process, you've opted to have a conversation with your principal. Before you go to the meeting, think about your audience and ask yourself, *If I were a principal who spent a long time working on what I thought was a good decision, what kind of critiques would I most likely listen to?* Would you listen to this teacher?

HOSTILE TEACHER: "So, this new tardy policy. No offense to whoever came up with it, but this is insane. There's no way this is going to work. It puts more work on me and students miss out on class time. Why weren't we consulted?"

What about this teacher?

CURIOUS TEACHER: "I have some questions about the new tardy policy. I know our old method wasn't working and needed revamping, and I'm glad we're revisiting it. I'm curious if there's a solution that works for teachers and students. What about this: Could we mark students tardy using the online 'tardy' feature in attendance so students don't miss class time and teachers aren't completing another form?"

Know when it's time to leave. I wish I or anyone else could make this decision for you, but knowing when it's time to leave is a personal decision with a lot of factors involved. Listen, I think that if you are confident in your emotional and physical stamina, it's honorable to stay at a school with weak or ineffective administration to try to enact change. But it is just as honorable to protect yourself, your mental health, and your career if you decide to seek out a different campus—*you will not be a good teacher if you are constantly stressed out by a toxic work environment.* Also honorable: If you have the skills to be a successful administrator, get certified and go be the type of boss you wish you'd had.

———

I know that last section may have shaken you up a little bit, but again, I assure you: Wonderful administrators *are* out there, doing the good work in schools across the country. I want to round out this chapter with a story about one of one of the most selfless administrators I know.

Just a week into the school year in August 2017, Hurricane Harvey flooded one out of every three homes in the Houston area. Just stop and think about that number for a second. Envision one-third of the people you know—your students, your friends, your family members, your coworkers. A third of a city of 2.3 million people had condemned homes and cars, but more seriously and more permanently, they experienced the trauma—adults and children alike—of witnessing the world they knew drown around them.

When Harvey hit, schools across the city sprung into action. We all saw the donation sites with diapers stacked twenty feet high, the GoFundMe campaigns to restock teachers' classrooms that were covered in hours, complete strangers "mucking out" houses for one another—tearing out any wet sheetrock along the water line and clearing out affected furniture and belongings. We saw the gift card drive for families affected by the storm and the meal chains for first responders from across the country who were working around the clock to help.

What we didn't see was what our principal was doing behind the scenes. To keep information as confidential as possible, my principal personally contacted each family in our school, including teachers, to check on our status. She kept a checklist with information on each family and their specific needs. She personally bought new clothes, shoes, backpacks, and supplies for students so they could return to school without feeling embarrassed, even going as far as to ask for their favorite colors and styles so that a small part of their life could feel normal.[3] She helped co-ordinate donations and special transportation for our students housed in unusual locations after the storm. She did all of this while keeping us posted on what we needed to know through constant e-mail communication but without compromising the dignity and privacy of our families.

And the only reason I know any of this is because I asked her. She didn't post her good deeds on social media. She didn't even tell us about all of this when we met as a faculty before school restarted. In fact, I suspect there's a whole heck of a lot more she did that she won't tell me. Because the welfare, privacy, and safety of her students, families, and teachers matters more to her than personal recognition.

May you one day find and work under an administrator like her. May some of you go on to be administrators like her. And may we all, in whatever kind of work we find ourselves, adopt a little bit more of this kind of leadership.

---

3   This part of what she did makes me cry every time.

Part III

When
Things
Get Tough

CHAPTER 11

Responding to the Students Who Challenge Us

There are three things you should know about Miguel.

First, Miguel was funny. Not funny in the way most seventh graders are funny, which is limited to their jokes about farting or puberty, but actually, truly funny. He had this quick, perceptive wit that was irresistible to his classmates and kept them squarely in the palm of his hand.

Second, he was adorable. Miguel had these huge, dark glossy eyes that lit up whenever he had someone's attention and that never seemed to get smaller, even when he smiled. With his doe eyes, unkempt hair, and thin neck supporting his head, he resembled an extremely tall, extremely adorable toddler that had wandered innocently into our middle school.

Third, Miguel made me absolutely miserable.

Miguel transferred to our school during my third year of teaching, which was a transitional time for me in my rookie years. As I mentioned in chapter 6, I spent my first two years

operating under the problematic classroom management philosophy that being nice was all I'd need to manage my students.
I believed that if I showed them that I loved them, they would
follow me with blind obedience. Having seen for myself how
hard this approach failed, I decided to run to the opposite end
of the spectrum my third year and abandon being nice altogether. Niceness had gotten me nowhere. In my first two years,
when I gave students extra time to do work, it never got turned
in. If I asked nicely for students to stop talking during class,
they'd look at me like I'd just made a neutral comment about
the weather, then continue their conversations. And if I let them
choose their partners or groups for an activity, I might as
well have walked out of the room altogether and handed them
my keys.

But at the start of my third year, I vowed things would be different. No more starry-eyed, overoptimistic New Teacher. Being
nice meant being weak. And if I had to choose between kids
liking me or kids learning, damn it, they were going to learn.
From August to February I held the line. I smiled minimally. I
cracked down on off-topic conversations and bad behavior so
hard, you'd have thought the kids in trouble had been caught
distributing methamphetamines.

And you know what? It worked. Kind of. Though behaving
like a stoic was unnatural and difficult for me, and though it
deeply bothered me to know that half of my students probably
hated me, kids were learning. I had control over my classroom.
I'd cut down on missing assignments and had way fewer kids
who dared to cross the line with me.

And then Miguel arrived.

Because of how common it was to get new students in my
school, I don't actually remember his first day in my classroom.

Kids came and went all the time—they'd have their schedule changed, move to a new apartment complex in the district, move out of state, or get sent to the alternative disciplinary school. Maybe half of the original class that started in August would be there in June. So, though I don't remember his first day, I do remember the first time I realized who I had on my hands. Ten minutes into my lesson, I spotted Miguel in the classic posture of in-class texters: His shoulders were hunched, his chin was to his chest, and the muscles in his thin forearms were pulsing slightly. I demanded that he give me his phone.

He sighed, rolled his eyes, grumbled something under his breath, and finally slid his hand out from beneath the desk. Using his thumb and forefinger, he lay a small paper cutout in my hand.

He'd drawn and cut out an iPhone. It was the right size, complete with rounded edges and little notches for the buttons on the side. He'd drawn in details by hand, the home button, camera, and screen featuring a text bubble with a simple message: "☺"

"It's paper!" a student at his table announced. The class erupted in laughter.

The next few weeks were filled with similar power struggles that grew in frequency and seriousness. I wasn't just struggling with Miguel; I was now struggling with an increasing percentage of the class. So many students who, before, had been compliant and quiet were now completely under Miguel's spell. They laughed at his jokes. They watched in raptured amusement when he calmly said, "Nope," to my directive to sit down, or turned the lights off before leaving class to go to the bathroom. Once, when I pointed out that he was out of dress code, he responded, "Aren't teachers supposed to wear closed-toed shoes?"

a cohort of students supported him, cheering and shouting, "Ohhhh! You got *burned*, Miss!" It didn't matter that teachers *could* wear open-toed shoes—my problem was much larger than whether he was right. He was the one who had control.

It didn't take me long to figure out that Miguel's misbehavior was largely due to all the idle time he had not doing any work for me. By not taking notes or completing worksheets, or even so much as putting a heading on a piece of paper, Miguel allowed himself plenty of time to do things like tape together his four fingers on each hand and ask me to call him Lobsterman.

For the first few weeks, I used every trick in the book with Miguel. I tried talking with him in the hallway. I tried separating him from others in the class. I even caved a little on my no-niceness policy and tried giving him special privileges, but he would quickly resume his usual antics. I thought maybe he was gifted and needed special writing assignments or tougher work to do, but he ignored those, too. I also considered the possibility that he didn't understand my lessons, but he understood them perfectly, answering any question I asked with ease when I'd challenge him. I questioned his other teachers at the school on how Miguel was performing for them and received similar reports to what I saw in my class. None of my colleagues or counselors had any magic trick or advice about how to get through to him. His disruptive behavior worsened and his list of missing assignments continued to grow.

In many schools, but especially in ones where administration is already stretched thin, when a child refuses to turn in work or participate, it's considered the teacher's responsibility; an instructional problem, not a discipline one. A teacher at my school could not refer a student to the office for not doing work or ignoring instructions. We also couldn't use failing as a deterrent, because in order to fail a student, you had to turn in extensive paperwork including a special form proving that you'd made at least three calls to parents, and the number listed for Miguel, like many of the other high-concern students at our school, was no longer in service. When I complained to administration that I felt I had no way of reaching Miguel because I felt my hands were tied in every direction I tried to turn, the response was a sympathetic sigh and, "Do the best you can."

So I did something I knew was shameful but that at the time felt necessary. I decided to ignore Miguel. For weeks, I directed my attention and focus to the other thirty-plus students in my class who were also behind—some of them multiple grade levels. If Miguel began an impassioned a cappella performance of "God Bless the USA" during instruction, I would talk louder. If he constructed an extra-long baton by stacking Crayola markers and used it to move the ceiling tiles above his head, I would quietly confiscate it and continue teaching. If he got out a Disney princess coloring book and crayons while the rest of his classmates were writing essays, I let him. I was angry that he was a distraction to the kids who worked hard and tried their best, but a part of me was also angry at myself for being a bad teacher. I was giving up on a child. I tried to justify this with all sorts of reasons: *I have thirty-three other students to worry about in this class. Nobody else can get through to him. His parents are impossible to reach. I have no other support on this.* The frustration continued to gnaw at me, but I ignored that, too.

During our poetry unit, about five weeks after Miguel arrived in my class, I reached my limit. Though I had become skilled at ignoring him, his tablemates had not. While the rest of the class worked on poems for a poetry slam coming up the following week, Miguel drummed out a beat with his pencil on his desk and sang a popular song whose lyrics were *Don't wake me up* but he replaced them with *Don't make me write.* Two of the girls seated at his table looked up at me, pleading with wide eyes for me to intervene.

"Miguel," I said. "You're being distracting."

"Ms. Treleaven," he said, imitating my voice so perfectly I almost laughed. "So are you." He continued singing.

"Meet me in the hallway," I said.

"Baby, if I wake and you're here still, gimme a pencil—"

"Now."

Miguel must have made some kind of face or gesture as he walked out behind me because I heard the entire class laugh. I was fuming. I shut the door a little too hard behind us. He was grinning.

"You have mandatory tutorials with me at three thirty-five after school," I said, so mad I was almost spitting out the words. "And I know you can make it because I saw your name on the list for soccer tryouts. I will e-mail Coach Stevens and will tell him you're taking a test for me, but if you don't show up I'll tell him to cut you from the team altogether because you're failing my class. Do you understand everything I've said?"

He crossed his arms and scowled. What Miguel didn't know was that it actually didn't matter if he was passing. Texas has something called the University Scholastic League, or UIL, which creates guidelines for student athletes—among the rules is that you need to pass all your classes—but Miguel didn't know that UIL rules only applied to high school sports, not to middle school. I hoped he didn't know that teachers weren't allowed to assign mandatory tutorials or to give any kind of official consequences, either.

"Three thirty-five," I said. "If you are one minute late, I'm sending the e-mail."

"What about fifty-nine seconds late?"

I ignored him.

Once my classes cleared after the 3:30 bell, I settled down at my computer to go through the mass of e-mails that had accumulated in my inbox during the day. I wasn't sure if Miguel was going to show. He hadn't shown up to any of my tutorials so far, but it was also possible that he thought I was bluffing with my e-mail threat.

But a few minutes later, I heard the door open. Miguel came inside. 3:33. I was relieved that he had shown, but mostly I felt what I usually felt when I saw Miguel: instant exhaustion.

"You're here," I said flatly. "Take a seat." He chose a desk as far away from my desk as possible and slid into a seat. He leaned back, cracked his knuckles, and stared ahead at the wall opposite him.

"Get out a sheet of paper and a pencil."

"I don't have one."

"Which? A pencil? Paper?"

"Either." He turned to me to say this, then returned his gaze to the wall.

I exhaled sharply through my nose, grabbed a sheet of paper and a pencil, and headed over to sit next to Miguel.

"You haven't started your poem yet, correct?" I asked. He shook his head and continued to stare into the space ahead of him.

"Okay," I said. "Let's start by brainstorming. Do you know what you want to write about?"

"My life," he replied. I was surprised. It was like he'd actually been thinking about what we were doing in class. We had been reading a variety of poems and talking about their wide range of topics, and how they often boiled down to themes about life or humanity.

"Okay," I said. "Go ahead and draw a little circle on your paper and write 'my life' in the middle. You can organize your ideas by having them branch off of your topic."

He drew a circle, then set his pencil down. He didn't look up at me.

"Label it 'my life,'" I repeated. Since he drew the circle so willingly, I thought he just didn't hear me.

He kept his gaze down. And then, I got it.

His refusal to even write a heading on top of a paper.

His complete understanding of verbal questions.

"Miguel, do you have trouble reading?"

He said nothing.

"Do the letters mix themselves up or flip around?"

"Yeah," he said. "Both."

"Have you seen a special teacher for it?" Though I'm not a diagnostician, I wondered if he could have dyslexia or dysgraphia. It's not uncommon at low-income schools for children with dyslexia or speech impediments to go undiagnosed or untreated. Most low-income schools can't afford to have a speech pathologist or a reading specialist on campus, which means a professional might be shared across multiple campuses, limiting the number of children who can be tested, let alone treated. If they are tested and diagnosed with a learning disorder, it can often take months before the intervention begins.

"I started to at a couple of schools. But then we moved."

"How often do you move?"

"I don't know."

"Have you ever spent a whole year at a school?"

"Maybe. I don't know."

I thought for a moment. Miguel drummed his fingers over the paper. My anger softened, but even though I knew he most likely was and had been struggling with reading and writing difficulty for years, it was still hard for me to do an immediate 180. When I looked at him, I saw how he'd caused my entire classroom to lose respect for me. I saw my students who cared about learning being distracted by his antics. I saw time—mine and my students'—wasted. I had lots of students with learning disabilities who didn't make my teaching life miserable.

"I'm sorry," I said. "That must be really hard."

He said nothing.

"Okay," I said, grabbing his pencil. "You talk, I'll write."

A half hour later, Miguel was sitting at his desk, recording notes verbally using his iPhone's voice memo feature. I'd written his initial notes for him, then shown him how to use his phone to continue on his own while I worked at my desk. Every once in a while, I'd catch his notes. His poem was about a TV. A kind of bizarre choice, but then again, this was Miguel.

"Miss? Can I go?"

Miguel was standing at my desk with his backpack on. I looked at the clock. It was already 4:20. The activities bus that dropped kids off from afternoon sports or tutorials would leave at 4:30.

"Oh, yeah. Sorry. I lost track of time."

He turned to leave.

"Wait, Miguel," I said. I paused. I felt the instinct I'd been pushing down all year. *Be a good teacher.* "Do you want to come in tomorrow morning? If you want, I can write down what you have done of your poem for you."

I waited for him to blow off my offer, make a joke, scoff.

"Okay." He stretched his thin arms out on either side and yawned.

"Okay." I smiled. "See you tomorrow." He turned halfway before opening the door.

"See you, Miss."

The next morning, I heard my door open again. But this time, Miguel came striding through.

"Miss, I'm done with my poem." He had his thumbs hooked through the straps of the backpack he was wearing and was bouncing on his heels just slightly.

"That's great, Miguel," I said. A little spark of hope lit up in my chest. "Can I see it? I mean, have you recorded it?"

"No, but I can tell it to you," he said. "Can you write it down while I say it so I can turn it in for the poetry slam?"

I smiled. This was definitely progress.

"Absolutely. How about I type it and I'll print it out for you?"

I opened up a new Word document on my computer and turned on the projector so he could see it as I typed it. Even if he struggled to read it, I wanted him to have a visual of what he'd accomplished. I had a hundred other things to be doing to get ready for school that day, but at that moment, I didn't care.

"All right," I said. "Go ahead."

He began reciting the poem, facing the board where his words were projected. I typed away, then stopped and reread what he had said so far. Tears squeezed out of the corners of my eyes, the involuntary kind when beauty runs you over. I kept typing.

"This next one, can it be on a new line?" he asked, looking at the board.

"Yeah," I said. Our eyes met just briefly, but he kept reciting.

Tears ran onto my neck as I continued typing. I felt crushed. I felt a tremendous, aching compassion replace what had only a day ago been frustration and apathy. The feeling was largely my own shame for how I'd handled Miguel and the frustration of realizing what a better teacher could have accomplished with him. But there was also an emerging awareness of the system that had allowed this to happen. This system had failed to meet Miguel's learning needs and had given me thirty-plus kids per class and expected me to pass all of them despite the fact that they were all behind. The system knew it was churning kids out into a world they weren't ready for. That system made it easier for me to be cold than to be compassionate, and it definitely made it harder for me to know my students or their gifts deeply unless it was accidental, like it was right now. The system was designed to keep my students down, and I'd done exactly what it had asked.

Miguel finished reciting. "Okay, that's all."

When I finished typing up the last line, I grabbed a Kleenex from my desk and pressed it into my eyes. I heard soft footsteps as Miguel approached me at my desk.

"That is a beautiful poem," I said. I tossed my Kleenex in the trash and looked up. He was grinning.

"You like it?"

"I love it. It's beautiful, Miguel."

We just looked at each other for a few moments, smiling.

"I made you cry, Miss," he said gently.

We both laughed.

"I'm going to tell everyone in class that I made you cry," he continued. "You know that, right?"

"You can do that," I said.

"I'm just kidding," he said. Then, he leaned closer to me,

widened his eyes so that I could see the full, dark circle of his irises, and whispered mock-conspiratorially, *"I shall tell no one."*

I laughed again and looked at the time. The first bell would be ringing soon.

"Thanks for coming in today," I said. "And listen. I'm sorry."

"For what?"

"I just haven't been a good teacher to you," I said, aware of what a huge understatement it was. "Or a good person." There was so much else I had to say.

"Nah, Miss. That's hyperbowl," he said, intentionally using the pronunciation I'd taught my students to avoid at all costs for *hyperbole.*

He was grinning.

If I got to choose the ending to our story, Miguel would have won the poetry slam the following week. I would have connected him with a dyslexia support teacher who was somehow able to bypass the system that split specialists between three different schools and would be able to work with him every day, making huge strides in his literacy and learning strategies to work with his challenges. After he left my class in June I would get yearly updates from him about his most recent successes, and we'd both say how that day with the poem changed everything.

But that wasn't our ending. Two days later, a student aide walked in my class during my conference period with a withdrawal form for me to sign for Miguel. I was shocked. He hadn't said he was moving. The poetry slam was less than a week away.

"Is he there—in the office?" I asked the aide. I wanted to say goodbye.

"No," she said. "I don't think he's here. He wasn't in my first-period class."

"Oh," I said. I scrawled my signature on the form and handed the clipboard back. She looked at the form.

"You forgot to initial this part," she said, pointing at the very bottom of the form. "If he has anything he needs to return to you, or whatever. Like, books and stuff."

"Oh, right, of course," I said, holding out my hands for the clipboard and wondering briefly, childishly, if not signing my initials would keep him from leaving, and wishing we could have pre-withdrawal withdrawal forms, giving us enough time to say the important things we needed to say and just hadn't found the right moment yet.

This is his poem:

> *The remote hates me.*
> *When I want to change the channel,*
> *It won't let me.*
> *It makes me watch whatever is there.*
>
> *And when I want to change the channel,*
> *It changes and won't go back.*
> *I don't get to know how the movies end.*
>
> *There's just so much static and noise,*
> *It's not even worth watching.*
>
> *Life is the remote.*
> *The TV is me.*

Teach long enough and you will come across a Miguel.

Actually, substitute for half a day and you will probably encounter a Miguel.

They're easy to spot. They're the boundary-pushers, the insti-
gators, the critics. They may struggle with learning or they may
be smarter than everyone in the room, including you. You'll
know them by how calm your class is in their absence. They're
the reason you need a glass of wine the size of your head by Tuesday afternoon.

These students are particularly difficult for new teachers who
are still working to get a handle on general classroom management and instruction. To throw in a student who makes it even
tougher to do all those things is enough to drive anyone to a
full-on meltdown.

But teach even longer and you'll learn how to connect with
the Miguels. This doesn't mean they'll necessarily be like putty
in your hands—after all, we're talking about the more rebellious
students here—but you'll get to see how their questions and
boundary-pushing help stimulate really strong classroom discussions. You'll see that their criticisms, with the appropriate
delivery, are often insightful observations on how things can be
better. You'll see how their skills as activators can get others
talking, participating, and on task. Teach long enough and you'll
be able to uncover the treasure that students like Miguel are and
have been all along.

Every situation and every child is different, but here is some
advice to meet you where you are:

1. Believe that the students who challenge us are amazing in their
   own way. Sometimes this is an easy thing to believe, while other
   times it takes some muscle. It's normal to get caught up in
   hopeless feelings occasionally, but remind yourself that within
   each of your students there is a gold mine, even though it

might be buried below the surface. I have never, ever liked a student less as a result of getting to know them. The whole reason I'm sharing this story about Miguel is that I don't want you to miss out on an absolutely critical opportunity to connect with your students and give them what they need the way I missed out on Miguel.

2. Understand that the students who are the toughest to handle are often the ones who are struggling to handle their own challenges. It might not be something tragic or dramatic—a lot of times people working in poor schools assume that all mischevious children have terrible home lives. It could be something as simple as being bored, which *is* a type of challenge. In my experience, most of the kids who have made my teaching difficult are kids who are going through something personally that they can't or don't know how to fix. Which leads me to my next point . . .

3. Know that it's not your job to "fix" them. It's not your job to dissolve poverty, cure mental illnesses or addictions, undo learning disabilities, or solve familial disputes. But it *is* your job to remember that these kids likely have been or are going through something difficult, to stand beside them and support them in whatever ways you can as they navigate these challenges, and to use that to drive your work with them instead of giving up.

4. Ignoring never works. I read in more than one book on classroom management that ignoring attention-seeking behavior is effective. And while there is a small nugget of truth in the fact that we shouldn't *encourage* attention-seeking behavior by arguing or reacting negatively, I think way too many

teachers—including myself—extend this advice to giving up on some level. I can't think of a time I've seen a child driven into submission by being ignored. In fact, if anything, I've seen it ramp up their behavior and lasso other kids into chaos.

The alternative to ignoring, then, is to notice them. Whether they need more practice with class routines or you need to put more muscle into building a relationship with that child, lean in.

5. Know that it's always worth being kind, even, but especially, when it's the hardest thing to do. The system we're in doesn't care about your personal needs. It doesn't care about teacher burnout. But don't allow the system to let you become the kind of teacher I was to Miguel. However long you're in this game, whether you stay in it for one year or for sixty: *Follow your instincts about what the best teacher version of yourself would do.* Listen. Be vulnerable. Laugh. Lead with kindness and firmness, not fear. Perhaps Miguel's greatest gift to me was the reminder that it's always better to teach (and live) this way.

6. Don't expect a Hollywood narrative. It would be so nice to live out the silver screen version of teaching: You go through a few days or weeks of hard work and *bam!* you've transformed the school's most notorious troublemaker into a Harvard-bound model student. But this is rarely the way it happens in real life. Sometimes you will see change quickly, sometimes you will see change build slowly, sometimes you won't see the fruits of your labor until years later when you get ambushed from behind at the grocery store and you wonder briefly if this is the end of your life before you realize it's a bear hug from a former

student. And maybe other times you won't see any change at all, but that will only be because the growth is taking place in a way assessments can't measure. But no matter if you get to see the change or not, believe that it's happening, and that it's worth the work you're putting in.

7. Reach out to other teachers. It doesn't always happen, but sometimes other teachers will have effective ways of reaching students you're struggling with. Ask them how you can better connect with the student in question and observe the class period that teacher has that student, even if it means getting coverage from your administration. Hopefully your administration is impressed by and supportive of your request. If they're not, point them toward this paragraph in this book in which I take a moment to remind administrators that THEIR JOB IS TO SUPPORT TEACHERS AND TO GIVE THEM EVERY AVAILABLE OPPORTUNITY FOR GROWTH.

Other good resources for new teachers are the coaches, band directors, theater or choir teachers, or other leaders at school who might hold a different relationship with the student than you do simply because of their subject area. A student might be more motivated to behave in your class if they know you're in communication with the person in charge of their tryouts or upcoming game, competition, or concert. This isn't to say you should use this as a threat like I did with Miguel and his soccer tryouts, but having support from another leader can help keep your head above water, so to speak, as you navigate building a relationship with a tough student.

————

As of the writing of this book, I'm working at a public, district-created school for highly gifted students, where I work with many students who share a lot of similarities with Miguel. These are the inquisitive, challenging, scary-brilliant minds who will point out every typo in my instructions, often take classroom discussions to a place that makes me cringe, and will find every last loophole in my rubrics. And I'm telling you: I adore them.

Sometimes I wish I could go back in time and redo my rookie years with the knowledge I have now. But part of why teaching has become so sweet is because of the struggle it took to get here. Part of why I work so hard now with my difficult students is because I had to understand how poorly I responded to Miguel and let that regret drive the way I taught in the future.

Be kind to yourself in this process. Give yourself permission to struggle, to not have it all figured out. And remember: The students who challenge us are our best teachers.

CHAPTER 12

Persisting Through the Worst Days

I don't remember the first time I cried during my first year of teaching. Maybe it was two weeks in, when the exhaustion really started to catch up with me. Maybe the first time I cried about teaching was on my way home, or while talking to my mom on the phone, or on a Sunday thinking about the week ahead. I don't remember.

I do, however, remember the first time I cried under my desk.

It was well into the fall semester of my first year, a time of year I would later diagnose as DEVOLSON, the Dark Evil Vortex of Late September, October, and November, a time that for me and many other teachers is one of the most taxing due to a combination of factors involving the transition from summer, a lack of breaks, and beginning-of-year boundary-pushing. But back then, I didn't have a word for DEVOLSON. All I knew was that I was miserable, struggling, and definitely not the only one feeling this way.

That fateful day, I remember feeling like a student watching the last fifteen minutes of fourth period tick by on the industrial clock above my door. When I'd felt upset before, I'd managed to wait until I got home to cry, or at least made it to the privacy of my car in the parking lot, but I knew today wasn't one of those days. Knowing that even opening my mouth might unleash the pressure cooker of sobs building in my throat, I nodded affirmatively to all student questions to avoid speaking.

"Ms. Treleaven, can I write in highlighter instead of pencil?"

Nod.

"Miss, can Yesenia and Rachel and Emma help me get my binder from Mrs. Taylor's room?"

You need three people to help you get your binder? Nod.

"Um . . . that essay that was homework? I left it at home."

Nod.

"Is that . . . okay?"

Nod.

When the last student left for lunch, I turned the lights off and paused just before opening the door to the hallway. I had planned on crying in the bathroom, but now I was reconsidering. What if I ran into another teacher or an administrator in the staff restroom? Half the faculty would know by the end of the day that the New Girl was crying. Or worse, what if students passed me in the hallway on my way back and saw my red eyes and swollen face? I couldn't risk being seen by anyone as weak; a wounded jackal limping among a lion pride.

I turned and faced my empty classroom. Without the buzzing of fluorescent overhead lighting or thirty-plus other noisy, shouting humans, it seemed like a completely different space. The sun was on the other side of the building now, so even though it was sunny and bright outside, the light filtered in blue and shadowy. It looked like a cave.

Yes. I would cry in here.

After shutting and locking the door behind me, I slipped off my shoes and crawled into the space under my desk. *Okay. You're safe now.* I pulled my knees to my chest and began to cry, the no-tissues, eyes squeezed shut, gulping-for-air type cry that comes when you've been holding it in for hours and finally have a break.

Did any of my teachers growing up do this? I wondered.

I heard a knock at the door. If my current breakdown had been a few weeks earlier in the year, I would have jumped up to open the door, thinking it was an administrator who needed to talk to me or a student who forgot their binder or a fellow teacher with a question. But, like many strange personality changes I'd taken on since I started teaching, I ignored my instinct to do the right thing and find out who needed me. I was in survival mode, and right then, surviving meant not answering the door.

Whoever it was didn't knock again. I picked my head up and rested my chin on my knees. From the small hole in the side of my desk, I could see part of my classroom window. *From here it looks all right,* I thought. The sky outside was so bright and cloudless it looked artificial—like you could scrape off the blue with a spoon—and the light made the orange and red vinyl leaves I'd stuck on the window from the teacher supply store glow like stained glass. Teaching looked beautiful, easy from my little porthole. It looked the way I thought it would be.

I ran through the day. Where had my meltdown started? Today had been a struggle, but it had been no more difficult than my other days of teaching so far—I couldn't pinpoint a certain student, a particular failure, an unexpected obstacle that had led me to crawl under my desk and cry. It wasn't like that. Instead, it was more subtle and massive, a great aching sensation

206 • Love, Teach

I'd felt building for weeks the way gathering clouds build to form a hurricane. It was an accumulation of things.

It was the instructional coach who last week insisted that a 56 percent average on the latest assessment of my students was fine, and that I was doing a great job and should stop worrying.

It was the student who said, "Why did our class get a 56 percent and Mrs. Black's class got a 86 percent? Are we dumber? Or are you a bad teacher?" And I asked how the student knew these numbers and he said it was posted in the hall on a huge chart with all the teachers' names and their class periods. I checked, and he was right.

It was writing an office referral for a student who said, "I'm not doing this shit," and having that student return triumphantly to class and announce, "I didn't get in trouble."

It was reporting this response later to that same administrator who said, "Do you know how many students would be in trouble if I gave out consequences every time a student was uncooperative?" And it was the big, bad feeling: *No one is going to help me do this.*

It was the growing realization that half of the home phone numbers listed for students on the computer system were disconnected, and that no administrator could give me a concrete answer about what I should do if I can't contact a parent.

It was reading journal entries from students that, legally, I had to hand over to the counselor, situations I would never have imagined having to face as a thirteen-year-old.

It was looking at my to-do list in an Excel spreadsheet that I'd made to prioritize tasks and estimate how long they'd take and realizing the total for the week was fifty-one hours. Not including the eight hours I would spend each day teaching.

It was everything. Individually, maybe, I could have tackled these problems. But all together it felt impossible. All together it felt like too much. What if it wouldn't get any easier? What if it could actually get worse than it is right now? Up until this point, I had been a steadfast optimist, clinging to positivity because positivity had always worked for me, just like hard work had always worked for me, or asking for help had always worked for me.

I checked my watch. I had ten minutes left of my lunch break. I lowered my head back onto my knees and thought, *This is so hard, this is so hard, this is so hard.* And I let myself cry.

New teachers need to know that in a lot of ways, the first year (or sometimes two) is like a grieving process. You are grieving the death of a person you thought you knew.

The self who used to be in control of your surroundings.

The self who always had easy, accessible, work-through-able solutions to problems in your life.

The self who was able to get the hang of anything—difficult professors, a conditioning class, the subjunctive in Spanish—after a few weeks.

The self who believed you were indestructible.

Of course, these are all false selves. None of us are in control of our surroundings. None of us have the solution to everything or can master everything immediately. But that doesn't make the grieving process any less difficult.

Like most grief, the grieving process in teaching looks more like a giant scribble than a neat line. One day you might think, *Wow, I'm killing it today—I must be on the upswing!* and the next you might feel completely inept. One day you might celebrate a successful lesson on polymerase chain reactions and the next your students can't tell you what DNA is. One day you will think it's impossible for you to love your third-period class any more than you already do and the next you will consider walking out the door during third period, climbing into your car, and driving to New Jersey, where you will then get on a ferry to Norway, change your name, and never again mention this period of your life.

Like the grieving process for a loved one, everyone's grief looks different. Some people take longer than others, and some have a more difficult journey than others. Some reach out for support from friends and family, some look inward through meditation or prayer. Some seek solace from experts in person or from books, some do a combination or find other forms of self-care (more on that in chapter 14). Don't judge yourself by comparing your struggle to that of other teachers—especially not ones at other schools. Administration, support, funding, bell schedules, all of these can create completely different experiences. Trust me, I've seen it myself. But even at your own school, don't expect to see other teachers crying in the teacher's lounge or posting pictures on social media of how badly their lesson failed. It's important to know and remember that just because you don't see someone else struggling doesn't mean they're not struggling, too.

Parts of me died in my first few years of teaching—parts of me that I honestly miss—but I had space for new, better versions of myself, ones that are better equipped to be a teacher and a person in this world. It was ultimately one of the most positive and transformative experiences of my life.

Today I am empowered by the fact that I have control of the way I respond to my surroundings, even if I don't have control of my surroundings.

I understand that some things have easy, accessible solutions, and some have giant, intimidating solutions, but that all of them are worth fighting for.

I see and celebrate the value in struggle and I teach my students to do the same.

I know I am destructible and I make it a priority to practice self-care.

I recognize my perfectionist tendencies, but remember to stop and breathe and think, *I'm enough. To work hard, to care deeply, to fight hard, to take care of myself: This is enough.*[1]

My Top Four DEVOLSON Survival Strategies

DEVOLSON stands for the Dark, Evil Vortex of Late September, October, and November, a term I coined for a time of year that is particularly challenging for me and a lot of other teachers. This season is a perfect storm of exhaustion, beginning of the year's paperwork, and adjusting to new personalities, all without any significant breaks until Thanksgiving. You'll try to "unlock" your classroom door with your car fob. You'll pour your coffee into a candle jar instead of a mug. You'll call your loved ones by your students' names for *weeks*.

Though it threatened my sanity more than once, when I finally had a word for DEVOLSON, this time of year became much more tolerable. With a little planning, you can make DEVOLSON work for you. Here's how:

1) Schedule fun into your calendar. Whether it's a weekend get-away or even just a weekly TV show ritual with friends, having

---

1 *I am enough* is a battle call from author/researcher Brené Brown. If you haven't read *The Gifts of Imperfection*, consider it required reading for becoming a teacher.

things to look forward to outside of school is a great way to maintain balance in an otherwise shaky time.

2) Make copies of all your keys and hand them out to responsible people. Seriously, a very common symptom of DEVOLSON is locking yourself out of your car, your home, anywhere with a key, really.

3) Have contact information for a good mechanic, contractor, and repair expert ready. Everything you have will break during DEVOLSON. Sorry.

4) Keep a running list of all the hilarious ways your exhaustion manifests itself and laugh with other teachers about it. A reader once commented that during DEVOLSON, she drove all the way home before remembering she left her husband at the grocery store. *Her husband.*

....

I was right about what I wondered on that first worst day: What if things actually got worse than they are right now?

They did.

But they also got better. Much better.

Here's the thing: You will not get to the good stuff in teaching if you don't trudge through the bad. What I learned under the desk is that you must let yourself feel. You have to allow yourself to go to those dark places where you want to quit, and to the even darker places where you begin to think that justice is an illusion and that our entire education system is in flames. Most of us aren't taught to sit with bad feelings; we're taught to ignore them or distract ourselves or stuff them down. Researcher and author Brené Brown says it best in her book *The*

Gifts of Imperfection: "We cannot selectively numb emotions; when we numb the painful emotions, we also numb the positive emotions." If you don't allow yourself to feel the painful stuff in teaching, you won't be able to enjoy the great moments, either.

I didn't know this wisdom, of course, on the first day I cried under my desk. I thought teaching would always be this hard, scary, and hopeless. I thought my feelings were reality, and that I really was a failure and weak. But I also didn't know that by crying under the desk and thinking, *This is so hard, this is so hard, this is so hard,* I was actually doing the right thing. I was letting myself feel. Often, growth is happening at the very moment we think we're breaking.

The Love, Teach Four-Step Bad-Day Recovery Plan

We all have bad days. Sometimes you can narrow it down to specific events, like you didn't know your document camera was positioned in a way that projected your cleavage onto the board instead of a passage you were annotating, or sometimes it's just a whole slew of built-up feelings that are difficult to pick apart. No matter the situation you find yourself in, here are my tips for recovering from a bad day.

1) Leave on a good note. Before you leave for the day, contact a parent with a positive message about a student's behavior or progress. I promise you'll feel better. I also like to read over cards and letters from former students and parents (I keep mine in what I call my Happy Binder).

2) Do one good thing for each of your five senses. I think that by covering all my senses, I trick myself into thinking I've cured

my whole self. Blasting Missy Elliott hits, looking at my baby animal Pinterest board, lighting a candle, getting in my softest pair of pajamas at 5 p.m., and sipping an ice-cold can of Trader Joe's wine typically does the trick for me.

3) Send your thoughts somewhere else for a bit. Chances are you've already reflected on why you've had a bad day and where you can improve, so now, give your mind a chance to wind down. Meditation and mindfulness can sometimes be overwhelming if you feel like your brain doesn't have a shut-off valve (me). So a visualization exercise I find helpful is taking each thought as it comes (*I don't have my lesson plans done. I should have said* this *in my e-mail instead. My observation totally tanked.*) and, in my mind's eye, send it off in its own little paper boat down a nice little river. It lets me acknowledge each thought and the fact that I'll return to it later—just not right now.

4) Go to bed early. I promise it'll be okay if you don't get your to-do list done before you go to bed. If you've had a rough day, the best thing you can do for yourself is to rest. Maslow before Bloom's, y'all.

You may decide after a bad day, or after many bad days, that teaching isn't for you, that you will be an advocate for kids and for public education in a place other than the classroom. That's okay. Honestly, I admire teachers who choose to pass the torch rather than continue teaching when they know they're not doing the best job they can.

But something to consider on your worst days is that, if you decide to stick with it, your best days are coming. If I could go back in time to that day, unlock the door, and go find the frightened and tearful me under the desk, I would tell her this: It will get better. I would remind her that for every moment of teaching that will send her under her desk, there will eventually be one that makes her heart feel like it will explode in a thunderous display of glitter and electric-guitar solos. I would tell her about Alejandra, a student she will have in a few years, who will begin the year refusing to read anything, and in March ask to borrow the sequel to the novel they just finished in class. I would tell her about leading writing workshops and listening to seventh graders talk about and critique one another's writing in a way that rivaled the college writing workshops she took.

The heart explosions, the under-the-desk cries, the into-the-bubble-bath cries, the onto-your-dog's-fur cries, this is all very normal in teaching. It's part of the roller coaster. And when I say roller coaster, I'm talking about the old wooden roller coaster in the back corner of the theme park, the one still there from the park's opening in 1951 that is still awesome but most people avoid because they think it's only a few loose bolts away from being condemned. Sometimes it's fun in a way that is actually fun, and sometimes it's fun in an "Oh, I'm actually going to die right now" kind of way.

And yet, somehow, despite the fear and the whiplash and the possibility of plummeting over the edge after a particularly sharp curve, once the ride slows to a stop, I find myself craving it—the thrill in my chest, the wind in my hair—and I get in line again and again and again.

Advice for the worst days:

1. **Sit through the storm.** Don't be afraid of sad or angry feelings. Acknowledge them, speak them out loud to yourself or to

someone else, put them down in writing, but don't try to pretend they don't exist. In my and most teachers' experience, the storms definitely get less intense and less frequent. And though they never disappear altogether, they do get easier to manage.

2. **When the storm is over, think small.** Once the worst part is over, think about how you can be proactive, but think small. Don't think, *Okay, how am I going to advance my students two to three grade levels in reading by May?* That will make you sad. Instead, think in terms of small, manageable tasks. *I'll ask the librarian tomorrow for her top recommendation for a high-interest book and bring it to my most reluctant reader,* or *I wonder if I could find that ghost story online about the dead bride and modify it for my classes.* (Fact: My middle school classes always loved reading ghost stories.)

3. **Don't take it personally, but take it seriously.** What I mean by this: When you have a really bad day or a particularly frustrating moment with your classes, don't equate it with your value as a teacher or a person. Examine it as an opportunity for growth. Instead of *Why do my students hate me?* think, *Let me look hard at this situation. Can I bring in a new procedure that might help? Who can I ask for advice about this? What can I do to foster a better relationship with this class?* The *what can I do?* attitude is not necessarily easier than despair, but it is so much healthier.

4. **Invest in your mental health.** When I'm president,[2] therapists will be free to all humans. But until then, I can't stress the importance of finding a good one and meeting with him/her

---

2   (I don't ever want to be president.)

regularly, especially during the tumultuous rookie years. Some districts offer therapy sessions as a part of their insurance plans, which is awesome. My therapist doesn't accept insurance, but she has been worth every out-of-pocket dollar I've thrown at her, even when I had to cut down every other part of my budget.

5. **Watch for the good things.** When things were really, really bad my first year, a friend's mom gave me this piece of advice I will never forget: *Watch for the good thing that will happen today.* It's great advice because it doesn't negate or minimize your pain, but it does help you ever so slightly adjust the lens you're using to look at your situation. No matter how bad a teaching day I've had, I can always pick out something good that happened—an eighth grader actually laughing at my grammar joke, finding a stash of Starbursts I'd forgotten about in my supply drawer, seeing the "tough kid" in school hold the door open for a younger class leaving to go outside. And if you go in looking for that good thing, you'll be much more likely to find it.

CHAPTER 13

Reframing Your Mind-Set

Let me tell you about a particularly low moment in my first year.

One afternoon, I reached my limit with a student named Marvin. His in-class smirking and sarcastic remarks had gone from slightly unnerving to the point that they made me feel like I could remove my own eyeballs out of sheer rage. I got permission from his mom to talk to him after school, and when he arrived in my classroom after the last bell, I directed him toward two desks I had arranged to face each other a few feet apart. He rolled his eyes and crashed into the desk violently, as if he'd decided, *Fine. I'll sit, but I'll sit the way I want to, dummy.*

"Marvin, I'd like for us to talk about the way class is going," I said.

Marvin folded his arms, looked out the window.

"I would really love it if we could work together. You could be a really big help to me, you know."

He blinked.

After a few more tries on my part, Marvin made it abundantly clear to me that he wasn't going to participate in a conversation, so I began to grade papers in front of him. Twenty-five minutes later I looked up and he was crying. I softened. "Is it something at school?" He shook his head no. "Something at home?" He didn't say anything. "Is there anyone you can talk to about it?" He wiped his eyes with his sleeve.

"Marvin," I said. I paused for a few moments, gathering my words. "If there's one thing I want you to understand before you leave today, I want you to know that I care about you. Not just how you do in my class but as a person." These weren't empty words—I meant it. I didn't care at all for Marvin's corrosive attitude, but I cared about him. Marvin stared out the window, but I know he heard me.

"You can go now," I told him. I thought maybe this was where we'd have our breakthrough. Maybe he would burst into tears and begin to break down the walls he'd put up around himself. Or maybe the shift would more subtle, like, just before leaving, he would look at me with a heartfelt expression and say simply, "Thank you."

He didn't do that.

Marvin got up, threw the desk he'd been sitting in on its side, then slammed the door. (Well, he would have slammed the door, but it was one of those time-release ones that just kind of make a *shhhhh* sound as they close very slowly. But I could tell he wanted to slam it because his skinny arm bounced back with the force of his near-slam.)

Maybe better teachers would have gotten up, run after Marvin, dealt with the conflict then and there, said something like, *No. I can't let you leave upset like this. Let's work this out.*

I just put my head down on the desk. It felt good, cool on my face.

You are the worst teacher ever.

I don't know if that was the first time I had that thought. In fact, I don't know if I thought it consciously. But I definitely felt it. Feeling—*believing*—you're the worst at something is a physical feeling. It feels like you're shrinking.

I decided to finish grading and head home. After an hour and a half or so, once the stack of papers in front of me dwindled down to zero, I migrated over to my computer. There's a saying in the education world that a teacher's work is never done, and it's true. I had a hundred other things I needed to get done yesterday, but I decided entering these grades into the online gradebook was the last thing I was going to do that afternoon. I tried to rally: *Come on, self. Just type these in for each class and you will be done for the day.*

After typing in each grade one by one, I hovered my mouse over the Save button to submit the grades of my first-period class. This is when I decided to glance over the column and actually think about the numbers I'd been entering.

Three students made above an eighty.

Ten out of twenty-eight students failed the assignment.

Five students didn't even turn it in, even though it was an activity I assigned at the beginning of class and collected from each student (I'd thought) at the end.

So, I realized, according to this data, I could not prove that even fifty percent of my class minimally understood the material.

As my eyes ran over the gradebook column, I went to a bad place in my mind.

I'm never, ever going to be good at teaching.

All my students are going to fail.

Marvin hates me.

All my students hate me, probably.

It's too late for me to go back and reteach the parts of speech.

I've let everyone down.

I shouldn't be here.

The second they find out what a bad teacher I am, I'm going to be fired.

I bet administration is already talking about firing me.

Every single one of those thoughts were true.

. . .

Of course they weren't! Those thoughts weren't true on the day I didn't go after Marvin after he flipped a desk, and they weren't true on my worst day of teaching, either. They also aren't true about you.

I've had a lot of time to reflect on the way my brain processed and worked through the challenges of my first year of teaching. And while a lot of why the transition was tough had to do with my perfectionistic tendencies, I think it was also related to the fact that I did not have adequate preparation for the classroom I found myself in. I'd been prepared for a classroom where I could count on the people above me for disciplinary support. I'd been prepared for a classroom where all or most of my students came in able to perform at grade level. I'd been prepared for a classroom where I could call my AP if I felt overwhelmed, and then she or he would deal with any discipline problems swiftly.

When it turned out that the classroom I was given required way more work than I had expected, my brain assumed that the problem was me—*I* was bad—which is laughable. And though I joke all the time about my learning curve during my rookie years, in reality I was nowhere near a failure. You know what was true about me on the day Marvin flipped his desk over and stormed out of my room?

- I was trying so hard to improve my instruction and classroom management to get it where it needed to be. I was taking advice and constructive criticism wherever I could get it and welcomed it.

- I loved my students, even Marvin, and was personally and professionally invested in their success.
- I was tired because I was working hard at something I believed in and that mattered to me.
- Every day I was improving. Even if the learning felt imperceptible to me, I was taking what didn't work and either honing it or trying something new the next time.

And you know what? I think that's really all that makes a good teacher, at least in the beginning stages.

I've said it once and I'll say it a thousand times: Education as a profession tends to attract a good deal of perfectionists. And while we perfectionists are great for our hard work and dogged resolve to achieve, we're not always great at seeing reality through an accurate lens. In fact, sometimes we don't just mis-interpret reality, but we re-create it to fit an alternate narrative where we're not the well-meaning protagonist but the villain's pathetic sidekick—weak and powerless but still somehow ruin-ing everything.

But you're the protagonist, dang it. Not the problematic su-perhero tasked with "saving" children, as we've discussed earlier, but the kind, strong, clever protagonist, the kind who responds to conflict not by shrinking, but by creating a rising action.

In thinking about and talking through the harmful narrative perfectionists spin for themselves, I've been able to narrow down some of the recurring feelings that pop up for me and other teachers I know. If you've never felt any of these feelings, great! If you have, take a look at why these feelings are straight-up lies from your perfection-loving brain. (But please remember,

I'm not a mental health professional. I am here for solidarity and to share my experiences, not to provide treatment. If you find yourself struggling to function normally, especially with thoughts of self-harm, contact a mental health professional ASAP.)

I'm the worst teacher ever. Did you feed pot brownies to your kindergarten class? Did you pay your biology students money to set one another on fire using lab equipment? Do you regularly leave your students unattended to take smoke breaks outside the cafeteria?

No? Then congratulations! You are not the worst teacher ever.

Chances are if you're reading this book, you're not even someone I or anyone else would consider a Bad Teacher. The Bad Teachers are not bad because they're making mistakes, struggling with classroom management, or haven't mastered instruction. The Bad Teachers are bad because they don't think they're making any mistakes, or know they're making mistakes and just don't care. They're the ones who say things like, "There's nothing wrong with my teaching," or "It's the kids' fault—if the kids weren't so (lazy) (terrible) (disrespectful) . . ." or "I don't need professional development."

Just because you're not absolutely killing it yet doesn't mean you're the worst. The best runners in the world started out as babies falling on their faces a thousand times and wailing about it. Ask Usain Bolt's mom.

I'm never going to be good at this. Some teaching books say, "Just work hard enough and have a positive attitude and you WILL be good at teaching!" While I agree in theory, I also think that mind-set fails to account for a lot of different factors. A good percentage of teachers don't make it through their first year—not for lack of effort or positive attitude, but because teaching is an extremely complicated, nuanced beast, and the experience can be wildly different depending on where you are and what level you teach. So many people decide to leave teaching before they have a chance to master it, but that doesn't mean that they didn't work hard or that their positive attitude was insufficient.

I think a better way to focus your thoughts is to remind yourself that teaching is a practice. The learning curve is slow but steady, and if you keep at it and practice and take care of yourself, you will get to a place where you feel confident.

I know the natural question that follows this principle is, "But when?" I wish I could give you a time frame. I wish I could say that it happens for everyone in six months to two years, or that there is an app or a special watch you can wear that measures and tracks how well you are doing. If there was, you could watch your progress tick up and up every day—even on the bad days (because you're learning the most on your bad days).

I will say that no matter how many people told me I was a good teacher in my rookie years, I personally didn't feel like I was truly "good" until around year three. And that's not a bad thing. It just means that even when I didn't feel like I was the most effective teacher, I was focused enough on my mission and saw enough of my (slow) growth to keep going. Despite the areas where I struggled, my rookie years were a time of energy and bold creativity—I came up with ambitious projects that encouraged my students to write things like original songs or create movie posters, games I made up on the spot that mostly flopped but were occasionally thrilling. My team of first-year teachers and I organized a field trip for an entire grade level to go see *The Hunger Games* so they could make intertextual links between the film and the book. These small victories—things I'm still proud of today—are what kept me moving forward.

I'm going to get fired. Even up until a few years ago, nearly every time I got called down to the office by my principal, I assumed I was in trouble. My first year, I thought it was because I was going to be fired. Now, in my tenth, I've let go of that feeling for the most part, but I do wonder if they're finally going to crack down on me for sending in my attendance late or letting multiple students stand on chairs while wielding staple removers to change my bulletin boards for me.

And yet, every time I walk into the principal's office, I'm never in trouble.

In fact, I told my current administrator this fear of mine, and now he says on the phone the same thing he says to students when he pulls them out of class for a benign reason, "Will you come down to my office for a second? You're not in trouble."

Here's a completely made-up statistic: 99.8 percent of new teachers who think they're going to be fired for how bad they're doing don't actually get fired. First of all, in most states, schools are required to show that they tried really, really hard to help you before they're able to sack you. Second of all, you're probably not doing nearly as badly as you think you are. Even when I had the appraiser who said my class was so boring he fell asleep,[3] I didn't get fired.

The only teacher I've heard of getting fired for being ineffective was a kindergarten teacher at my friend's school. Despite repeated interventions for her to provide adequate instruction,

---

3   After his comment, due to my own stubbornness combined with a fiery distaste for his leadership style, I made sure any lesson he'd walk into in the future was more interactive and lended itself to asking for his participation ("Mr. Haynes, would you give us a noun for this sample sentence?"). After that, my scores in observations were more positive. And that, my friends, is how fear-based leadership works.

this teacher's daily agenda consisted of putting on back-to-back movies, punctuated by breaks to give the kids Little Debbie snacks or chips. (Which sounds kind of wonderful if you're an adult but really tragic if you're a child who doesn't know how to read and would also like to avoid Type 2 diabetes.)

Here's your mantra the next time you think you're going to be fired.

I didn't show twenty movies this week.

I didn't hand out oatmeal cream pies in place of instruction.

I'm probably not going to be fired.

All my students hate me. Well, this one is probably true. It's that natural onion deodorant you're wearing.

Just kidding. Students don't misbehave because they hate you. They misbehave because they don't have procedures, the procedures aren't working, you are still developing your relationships in the classroom, or you haven't quite figured out the balance between being firm and kind. Getting all that right may seem really daunting, but here's the good news! *They are all things you can work on.* Bonus: They're all things I talk about in this book!

The types of teachers students genuinely and deeply dislike are not the type of teachers reading this book. They're the teachers who are completely uninterested in changing anything about their class, methods, or approach for the benefit of their students.

It's too late to change things—the rest of this year/semester is going to be miserable. While it's true that it's easiest to implement rules and procedures from the very beginning of the year, it's definitely not impossible to make change happen at any point during the school year.

I know this is true because a few years ago I worked with a first-year teacher who started off without any rules and procedures.

After observing the familiar first-year chaos in her room for half a class period, I gently encouraged her to read the procedures section in *The First Days of School*. She had the exact same reaction I did when I first read it: Nope, not for me, teaching students how to do basic things like enter your classroom sounds robotic and weird. A month later, she came into my room on the verge of tears. "I feel like it's too late now," she told me. "I can't just press Pause and go back and teach procedures now that we've started the curriculum."

It was not too late. I sat down with her and made a plan. She would take two days off from her curriculum to teach students the most important procedures and have them practice them until they could do them perfectly. Then, for the next two weeks, in the time usually devoted to the warm-up, she would teach new procedures and/or have students practice the ones she'd already introduced. I helped her craft the way she would present her plan to administration, knowing that her appraiser would need to know what she was doing in the classroom. Here was her script: "I'm struggling with classroom management, and asked my mentor teacher to observe me and give me feedback. Together, we've crafted a plan to get things under control using research-based strategies and best practices. It uses some of my class time for the next few weeks, but it will be worth it in the time it saves me in the long run." Administration was on board, and things were sailing much more smoothly after that.

Here are some tips that have worked for me when I've caught myself believing a teaching lie.

Shifting Your Mind-Set

Talk to yourself the way you would talk to a friend. This is one of the simplest but most important pieces of advice I've ever received. Think about what you would do if your best friend came to you devastated after making a mistake at work. Say she works as a paralegal and she made a mistake in a briefing. What would you say to her? "Wow, world's worst paralegal right here! You should probably quit, dumb-dumb." Of course not! You would be kind, gentle, and encouraging because you believe in and love your friend. You would say what you believe about her and the situation, things like, "Everything's going to be okay. You are a smart, capable, butt-kicking paralegal and this is just a tiny hiccup in a successful career. This mistake doesn't define you." It may sound a little hokey (it did to me), but if the voice in your head is one of constant criticism and panic, talking to yourself kindly on a regular basis will be unbelievably refreshing.

Learn to identify what is true and what isn't. When you're struggling, it can be difficult to distinguish between reality and the reality you've created for yourself. My mom often has me refocus my thoughts when she hears me projecting my own insecurities onto a situation.

> **Me:** That teacher I work with hates me. I e-mailed to ask if she would please try to be on time to morning tutorials so I don't have to watch her students while I'm trying to prepare for the day, and it's been three hours and she hasn't responded.

> **Mom:** I think you might be creating a story that she hates you. What if she's following up on an e-mail from a crazy parent accusing her of excluding flat-earth theories from his instruction? What if she was working on a draft to respond to you and then got a phone call from her bank saying there were fraudulent charges on her card for $541 at a

pet store in Boston? What if she doesn't hate
you but is a little embarrassed to find out
you've been babysitting her tutorials students
and is figuring out how to respond?

Me: Oh, never mind. She e-mailed back and said,
"So sorry. Of course!"

Mom: ☺

In the same way, I think a lot of the things I panicked about during my rookie years were projections—feelings I had about myself that I placed on others or outside situations. If you believe that you are a failure or a bad teacher, you will find ways to interpret anything you come across as evidence that this is true.

A good rule of thumb is that if you find yourself using extreme language or all-or-nothing thinking ("All my students hate me," "I'm the worst teacher in the world"), chances are you're just being overly critical. And if you're still convinced you're the worst teacher or that your coworker hates you, ask yourself "grounding" questions tied to reality. Am I working really hard to improve? Do I care deeply about my students and the work that I'm doing? Am I learning, even if it looks messy and not at all the way I thought it would? If you can answer yes to these questions, you are doing just fine.

Think of teaching as a language you're in the process of learning. I remember expecting the learning curve in teaching to mimic other jobs I'd held where, after the first shaky week or two of folding children's clothes or shaping pretzel dough or getting kids to their camp activities on time, I was a pro. In reality, teaching was more like learning a language. It takes a year or more to learn the basics and years of complete immersion after that before you're fluent. This isn't to say that it'll necessarily take you years to be a good teacher—I know plenty of teachers who were good and even fantastic right out of the gate[4]—but it's far more helpful to think of teaching as a long process in which you're building skills and vocabulary every day instead of a single hurdle to clear.

Though we spend our whole day in a class full of children nine months out of the year, if you can't get out of a negative headspace, teaching can feel completely isolating. If you remember nothing else from this chapter, remember that no matter what you're thinking about, no matter what you're struggling with, no matter how unique your experience seems, no matter how many students fail a spelling test or defecate on top of your desk,[5] *you're never alone.*

---

4 It should be noted that even the teachers to whom I compared myself hopelessly in my first year look back at their own start and think, *Oh, I was a HOT. MESS.* I know this is a fact because that's an exact quote from a fantastic teacher I just texted.

5 Happened to a friend teaching middle school in another state. Thinking about that incident is a way I regularly recalibrate when I think I've had a bad day.

CHAPTER 14

Let's Talk About Burnout and Self-Care

One of the most common e-mails or messages I get as Love, Teach is from teachers who are thinking about quitting—either leaving the profession altogether or switching to a different school. I hear echoes of my own voice from years ago in e-mails and messages from teachers who are heartbroken and lost:

> *I'm not taking care of myself.*

> *I feel like I have to choose between giving teaching 100 percent and burning out or giving it less than my best and staying above water. The system makes it impossible for me to do my best.*

> *I love my school. I love my kids. I just can't do this anymore.*

In my time as an educator, I've thought about quitting hundreds of times. I can't tell you how many Monster.com Days I've had—days I've spent my conference period scrolling through online job postings because I'm not sure I can take another day of being a teacher. But Monster.com Days are fleeting. They're usually brought on by a relatively minor annoyance that eventually resolves itself. You eventually either decide that you actually do want to keep teaching or that quitting would be too much of a hassle. You go home and eat an entire frozen pizza by yourself and you live to teach another day.

Burnout is different. If Monster.com Days are the days you realize that the flame is dying; burning out is when the flame is long gone and all that's left is a handful of coals. Burnout doesn't usually happen with a bang or some kind of dramatic situation like a screaming match or a showdown. It's the final wheeze of a dying fire.

I've almost burned out twice in my time as a teacher. In both situations, it had nothing to do with any one incident. I was facing situations I'd dealt with countless times before, but it was a sudden moment of clarity like, *Oh, this is much bigger and sadder and more impossible than I thought it was.*

The first time I thought I'd burned out was in my second year of teaching, toward the end of the year. I had been planning a three-day, high-interest unit for my students using materials I paid for out of my own pocket and media I spent hours collecting and putting together. The project involved students learning more about themselves and their peers through personality tests; building up their confidence about the transition into high school with silly and serious movie clips I'd collected; and solidifying some social-emotional learning before the end of the year by discussing the connection between art and mood. I was calling it "Student Appreciation Week," because one of my students had joked during Teacher Appreciation Week, "Why don't we get one?" Before I even started planning this unit, however, I cleared my idea with administration, making sure we didn't have any assemblies or major field trips for those three days, and I'd been given the go-ahead. Then, less than a week before my unit was supposed to take place, we got a school-wide e-mail saying that two of the three days I had planned for Student Appreciation Week would be replaced by a school-wide party to celebrate the end of standardized testing for the year.

Now, I wasn't mad when I got this e-mail—I didn't believe that someone had sabotaged my plans or had intentionally chosen dates for the celebration that would conflict with my unit. Honestly, I was used to last-minute changes and communication mishaps. Plus, I knew that I'd planned poorly in choosing a week in May, when the schedule is particularly prone to last-minute changes. But I did hope that I could meet privately with one of my administrators to remind them of my unit and discuss the possibility of working something out—maybe letting me use two days of finals week to teach my unit, or allowing me to teach just one section of eighth graders who wanted to come see the guest speakers. I had spent my entire time at that school always saying yes to the most insane requests and staying silent when I disagreed, so I thought I was in good enough standing to negotiate a compromise. Instead, my administrator's response when I pointed out the conflict was to say, in front of two other teachers who happened to be in the office, "I'm sorry, who told you that you were so damn special?"

My feeling of burnout wasn't because I'd been told no. I'd been told "no" in some form every day of my teaching:

No, we don't have nearly enough counselors to meet with the students we have.

No, we can't give your class sets of books or the supplies you need.

No, we can't offer you disciplinary support; that's your job.

No, you can't have your conference period for the next two weeks because you need to be teaching tutorials during it instead.

I was used to "no," and had spent the past two years learning how to creatively respond to "no." It was way more than not getting my way.

I realized in this moment with my administrator that even though I'd done everything I'd ever been asked—including spending a lot of my time on campus on weekends and before and after school—I was not and would never be in the position where I would feel comfortable challenging decisions. The only acceptable opinion I could offer was *Yes, ma'am* and *I think that's a great idea.*

I realized that I hadn't been encouraged to be the English department chair my second year of teaching because of my leadership skills or charisma or teaching abilities but because I did what I was told to do without questioning it.

It became clear to me how this principal and others like her had gotten to where they were. When your leadership is based on fear and intimidation, when you've made it clear to the people under you that their questions will put them on the chopping block, or, at the very least, be met with some degree of hostility, your power becomes uncheckable.

I realized the truth that you can work hard, do the right thing, and be good at what you do, and still be treated as if you are undermining authority or cutting corners the first chance they have to cut you down.

I realized, for the first time in my sheltered and privileged life, what it was like to feel you have no voice or power.

After that incident, even though I suspected I was nearing burnout, I decided to transfer and try teaching somewhere else.

I chose an essentially identical school but that was in a district with a much better reputation for leadership and happy teachers. My plan was "One more year." I would give myself one more year at this new school to determine if I still wanted to teach. Luckily, the difference was huge. I trusted the leadership and felt valued and respected. Central administration was transparent and made it a point to be present in our schools—our faculty meetings, our classrooms, our professional development. Character education in addition to academic instruction was taught across the district. I felt like I was finally working under and with people who had similar values.

No school is perfect, of course, and I had my fair share of bad days. But bad days are an entirely different experience when you trust your leadership and have better access to resources. I didn't need to question leadership very often, and when I did, I was heard with respect and recognition of my professionalism, regardless of whether or not I got the answer I wanted.

What happened at this school was that I realized that even when administration is professional and capable, there are forces larger than our school or district at work that keep certain things dysfunctional. Over the course of my time there I realized that my rainy days weren't rainy days at all; that we were stuck under a huge, elaborate faulty sprinkler system that none of us could turn off: the system.

Eventually, this led to the second time I suspected I had burned out, a day about three years into working at my new school. The triggering event was that I personally walked another teacher's student to the office after she called me a bitch during a passing period. Later, I found out from that teacher that the student returned to class five minutes later with candy. When asked why she was late, the student reported happily,

"Some seventh grade teacher sent me to the office. I like it there." I realized then that I was deeply frustrated, but I had nowhere for my blame to go.

It wasn't the girl's fault for being disrespectful. If I figured out that the system around me didn't care whether I behaved perfectly or acted out—and more seriously, that the system would pass me to the next grade even if I did nothing the entire year—I think I might act out, too.

It wasn't the girl's parents' fault that they behaved disrespectfully. In my five years of teaching in inner-city schools, never once did I come across a parent of a child with behavior challenges who said, "What's the problem? I find disrespectful behavior acceptable."[1]

Though I think the administrator could have handled the situation differently, it wasn't his fault for not issuing a detention or suspension; he wasn't allowed. Everyone knew that our school was near the top of the list in the district for suspensions and write-ups, and that we'd been told months earlier that essentially there would be no more school-issued punishments except for extreme cases involving violence.

It wasn't the assistant principal's fault for being close with the girls, either. I won't ever fault a leader for caring about kids or for developing relationships with them, especially since, at the time of writing this book, I've never been a principal of any kind. I also can't say for certain whether the candy was from the assistant principal or someone else from the front office, but the optics alone were depressing.

---

1 Ironically (or maybe not ironically), I see that kind of reaction way more often in wealthy schools.

Again, it was the system.

I had thought that teaching was all about your administration—that if you could just find the right leadership, you could go ahead and start changing the world, ending education inequality, closing that achievement gap, ending poverty. But in this second moment of near-burnout, I realized that, no matter how hard I worked with the kids in my classroom year after year, I was voiceless in a system much larger than my district keeping them and me down.

I had a breakdown that night. I was face-to-face with something scary that I'd been refusing to see: I was depressed, and it was caused by a job that I loved fiercely, which served kids that I loved fiercely. I knew I wasn't taking care of myself, because taking care of myself felt impossible.

Even under an administration that I felt generally supported me, I had burned out.

I was terrified. So much of my identity was wrapped up in teaching, including my identity as the Love, Teach blogger. What would become of my blog and my readers if I left the profession? More critically, who was I if I wasn't a teacher?

One more year, I told myself again. I had one more year in me to figure this out.

I went to a few interviews at private schools. They were incredible schools with incredible people, but they didn't feel like the right fit. After one interview, I sat in my car with my head on the steering wheel, crying. Is this what I had to do to be able to do my job well? Teach at a school that felt more like a country club?

A few days later on a whim, I texted a friend who had left our school the previous year to work in a special school my current district started to meet the needs of its exceptionally gifted students only a few years earlier.

> Hey, friend! I'm struggling. Any chance your school needs a middle school English teacher next year? ☺

I saw the gray iMessage ellipses. She was already typing a response.

> Oh my gosh. I was seriously JUST thinking about you. We actually do! I'll call you after school! I'm so excited!

I went into the interview very hesitant, but left hoping that the principal and assistant principal would adopt me in addition to hiring me. They were incredible people, I knew immediately. The teaching role would be very different than what I was used to—teaching much smaller classes but with more preps—not just classes but separate, individual courses—than I'd ever had (five) as well as a fifteen-minute drive to switch campuses halfway through the day.

"I know it's a lot," my principal admitted, "but we want to be transparent about the workload you'll have."

"I'm in," I told them. *One more year,* I thought again, but this would be the last time. This year was the deciding factor.

My principal was right. It was a lot. It *is* a lot, because at the time I'm writing this, I still teach at that school. I definitely have more of a workload in the instructional sense: more planning, more prep work, more curricula to write and revise. The parents at this school are far more involved than anywhere I've ever worked, and navigating when and how to communicate with them was bumpy at first. And while I definitely deal with less severe discipline issues at this school, highly gifted children definitely come with their own unique challenges, including the need for me to stay not one step ahead of them but twelve.

But for me, this school was definitely the right fit. As in any school I've worked, my students—their quirks, their dreams, their fire—are the best part of my job. I have the autonomy to choose my own curriculum while still collaborating with other teachers to calibrate my instruction. I trust and deeply respect my administration, and I know they trust and deeply respect me. I don't have to take on roles that are beyond my realm of expertise. Here, I can actually focus all of my energy on teaching, building relationships with my students, and staying in contact with parents.[2]

Slowly, over several years of being at this school, little whooshes of air began to rush over the dying coals of what was nearly my burnout. First just a glow, then, little by little, I've come back to the fire I felt when I first started. I'm able to focus on the right things. I've built the kind of classroom and relationships with my students I've always wanted to have.

But even though I have landed my dream teaching job, it's important to note that teaching is not a cakewalk here, either. And even in a school with everything I could ever want on a professional level, I still have to be very careful about not exhausting myself, making sure I have a healthy balance between my work and personal life, and taking care of personal and financial needs while on a teacher budget.

---

2 Consider this another education advocacy moment—all teachers could feel this way if we had smaller class sizes, the type of compensation that brought in the best of the best, and policies that supported teachers—especially those in Title I schools—instead of making their jobs harder.

If you're a brand-new teacher or haven't started teaching yet, I want to stop here and assure you that I'm not trying out scare tactics here or trying to steer you away from teaching. Teaching is the most honorable profession I know, one that has undoubtedly changed my life for the better. And despite everything I've been through *I would do it all again.* I just want to be real about exhaustion, because I definitely didn't understand it before I started teaching. And when I began to experience it myself, what I did read online were articles with titles like:

- 11 Ways to Avoid Burning Out

- Teacher Burnout: Don't Become a Statistic!

- 9 Solutions to Teacher Burnout You *Haven't* Heard

- Thinking of Quitting? Don't, Because If You Do You're Not Only Failing Yourself, But Also Failing Kids

Here's what I wish I'd been reading:

- Wrestling with Burnout? I've Been There.

- 15 Ways Teachers Can Practice Self-Care

- Burnout Isn't Failure for Teachers: It's a Failure for Our Nation

- I Burned Out as a Teacher and Became a State Legislator with a Pro-Public Education Agenda

See what I'm getting at?

Here's the truth about burnout.

It happens. Sometimes you can keep it from happening. Sometimes you can't. But there is a lot of honor in giving everything you have to a cause you care about, no matter how long you spend doing it.

So, knowing all of this, if you are still willing to join me and millions of other teachers fighting the good fight, here are many ways to take care of yourself while you're teaching, whether you feel burned out or fired up.

Self-care *has* to be a priority. Way, way, way too many teachers don't take care of themselves.

Some have no idea they aren't taking care of themselves. Others have the wrong idea about self-care, thinking that it means practicing indulgence or selfish behaviors or trivial things limited to face masks. Still others believe a dangerous narrative about teaching, which is that we are supposed to be martyrs who lay down our lives, our health, our finances, everything for our students.

We are not martyrs. We are not radical missionaries who have decided to forfeit our money, families, and worldly obligations for the cause. We are professionals.

Weirdly, I think our society tends to praise people who neglect self-care. We love mothers who haven't showered in days, nonprofit owners who work seven days a week, teachers who stay at school until 8 p.m. But we should be worried about people who are neglecting their own wellness! You will never perform at your best—including teaching—if you do not also take care of yourself. Humanity's most revered servants—Ghandi, Martin Luther King, Jr., Desmond Tutu—achieved what they did because of their devotion to taking care of themselves through rest, prayer, solitude, or meditation.

You know by now that I am not a psychologist or a licensed anything (besides teacher), but here are some ways I've learned to practice self-care:

- Take care of your body. We all know that it's good to eat healthy and get plenty of exercise, but that can be really hard to do in a profession that already demands a lot of your body. A practice I've adopted during the most trying times in teaching is that if a healthy habit I'm trying to adopt seems too hard/overwhelming, I just try to take a step in the *direction* of a good thing. If I know I should go for a walk in the fresh air but the idea of working out after spending eleven hours on my feet makes me feel like crying, I'll take my dinner out onto the patio, turn off my phone, and breathe deeply for twenty minutes. If I know I should eat a healthy dinner but the thought of standing in my kitchen and chopping anything is completely unappealing, I'll swing by one of those stores that have healthy prepped meals on my way home. Baby steps are positive steps!

- Pay close attention to the way certain foods and activities make you feel. One thing that has made taking care of my body a thousand times easier is being aware of my mood. For example, I love bagels, but I realized I feel terrible and starving about two hours after I eat one. I hate waking up at 4:45 to work out before school, but I realized I feel amazing and have boundless energy when I do. Simply being aware of how I feel has made it easier to make choices that are better for my body. Does eating your lunch outside in the sun make you feel like a shimmering goddess afterward? Do it. Does a standing desk make you feel like you're standing on the TED stage giving an impassioned speech about your content area? Do it. (Having a fake microphone headset helps.)

- Rest. Sleeping well is incredibly important for teaching well. But apart from getting enough sleep each night, it's important to set aside time in the evenings and on weekends to really unwind. Pack a picnic and eat it at the park. Wander around a quiet museum. Work on a craft or nonschool project. I'll never tell you that self-care can't include screens, but I often feel way more rested when I peel myself away from my phone or TV.

- Taking care of your body includes taking care of your mind. Meditation, yoga, and mindfulness practices changed my life as a teacher. I'm not exaggerating. There's a reason schools across the country are adopting these practices for their students. Mindfulness practices won't erase the things that cause you stress, but they can help the way you respond to that stress and move away from internalizing or dwelling on it. How can you learn these skills? You can always take a class if you're more of an in-person learner, but there are a zillion apps, books, and articles out there that will guide you through any of these.

- Find a good therapist or counselor. I know I've mentioned this several times in this book already, but that's because I feel so strongly about having someone neutral to talk to about work, both to avoid putting a strain on your personal relationships and to have an objective view on the situations you describe. A therapist can also help you determine if your mental health is at risk and give you stress management techniques you might never have considered. Let's talk about cost. Again, some insurance plans cover therapy, but my therapist didn't accept insurance. If you find yourself in the same situation you have several options: 1) Talk to your insurance and see if they can work something out. Some companies have policies for out-of-network physicians/

therapists and are willing to work with you on getting the healthcare you need. 2) Rework your budget. It was totally worth it for me to cut down on groceries, entertainment, and other costs to go to therapy for a year. I got very creative with sweet potatoes, eggs, and black beans. 3) Space out your therapy appointments. If you can't afford to go every week, go once a month or maybe once a quarter. Also, I would recommend asking around with people you trust for a therapist, as web reviews haven't proven super reliable to me and other people I know.

- Practice relationship maintenance. When things get tough, it's really easy to let friendships and relationships fall by the wayside, but your support network is critical to your self-care. Don't let teaching destroy your safety net! Depending on what works for you, this might look like creating a fun weekly social routine, a daily text check-in, a monthly dinner party, or a whole host of other ways to connect with the people in your life who make you feel strong.

- Do what makes you feel powerful or alive. Think about what you do that afterward makes you think, *Man, I feel on top of the world.* Finishing an intense workout?[3] Making a really great recipe out of a cookbook for yourself or a group of people? Getting your house or apartment immaculately clean? Playing an instrument or seeing live music? Traveling? Learning a new skill? Make time for these things. (And if you're reading this and thinking, *But I have no desire to do any of the things I usually love doing,* see my earlier point about seeing a therapist or counselor.)

---

3   If so, you're crazy, but I'm happy for you.

Know that if you do burn out, it is not because you have failed. When I left my first school, I experienced a lot of guilt surrounding my decision. I felt like I was failing the students at my school and their community. I worried about abandoning them to a teacher who might not champion them as much as I'd tried to. But when you think about it, that kind of assumption is a little self-aggrandizing. It assumes two untrue things: 1) that nobody else could teach or love those kind of students the way you do, and 2) that your students are unequipped to be successful with anyone less amazing than you are. Often, leaving a school looks way more like passing the torch to someone who is totally fired up than it looks like a torch simply blowing out.

Another thing to keep in mind is that burnout isn't always permanent. Sometimes teachers need to step away into a different profession or a different school for a few years, recharge, and then they come back ready and energized to do the work they love so much.

If you do decide to leave teaching, there are so many ways to advocate for education and students without being a teacher. You can donate school supplies to teachers every year during back-to-school. You can tutor, mentor, or volunteer at local schools. You can run for school board or another public leadership position that desperately needs representation from former teachers. You can go into education policy and advocate for teachers and students, knowing what we're facing on a personal level.

I hope you'll stay in this race with me—it's the most important race there is. But know that stepping out does not mean giving up.

CHAPTER 15

The Road Ahead

Some parts of our lives we're able to predict and plot on neat graphs. If you lift weights regularly, you will get stronger. If you practice trombone every night for an hour, you'll be able to play more proficiently. If you eat buttery popcorn for dinner for three months straight, your doctor will hand you a pamphlet on bad cholesterol after your next blood panel. When I started teaching, I wanted my graph to look like like the first image that follows.

You can imagine, then, that I was very surprised when I became a teacher and realized, even when I did everything I was "supposed" to (i.e., work hard, love my students, go to professional development, learn from my mistakes) the graph is actually a scatter plot.

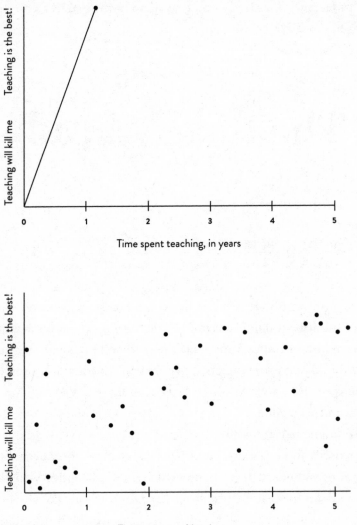

Time spent teaching, in years

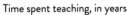

Time spent teaching, in years

In fact, if you zoom in and look at an individual week on the graph, it actually might look like this:

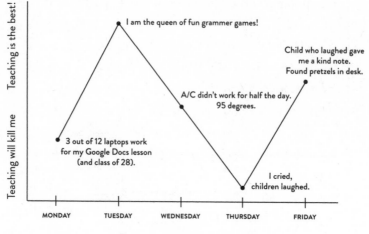

Teaching is the best! / **Teaching will kill me** (y-axis)

I am the queen of fun grammer games!

Child who laughed gave me a kind note. Found pretzels in desk.

A/C didn't work for half the day. 95 degrees.

3 out of 12 laptops work for my Google Docs lesson (and class of 28).

I cried, children laughed.

MONDAY · TUESDAY · WEDNESDAY · THURSDAY · FRIDAY

Time spent teaching, in years

When new teachers e-mail and tell me about how hard their first year is, or they ask me if my first year was my toughest year, or they ask me when things will get better, the answer is complicated because the graph is a scatter plot and not a straight line.

It *will* get better.

It might also get worse.

I don't think it's unoptimistic or "negative" to expect that teaching will be hard. I went into teaching thinking that it would be exclusively awesome (or maybe hard for some people, but not for *me!*), but that mind-set, of course, gave me some crushing disappointment in my rookie years. I think the right approach is to go into teaching knowing that some days are going to be really, really great, but that others are going to be really, really hard; to prepare for the best *and* the worst without focusing your expectations on either. That way, when the really hard days come, you can say, "Ah. Here it is. Maybe I didn't know how hard it would be, but I knew this was coming and can now handle it with the preparation I've done," instead of "WHAT IS HAPPENING TO ME?! WHY AM I NOT WINNING ALL THE TEACHER AWARDS? WHY DO I FEEL SAD ALL OF THE TIME?"

I've talked about the hard parts of teaching quite a bit in this book. I've touched a bit on the triumphs of my rookie years, triumphs that came after a tough lesson or a difficult challenge. What I haven't talked about in teaching is its arresting, all-encompassing, sometimes bordering-on-unbearable beauty.

I did this intentionally, because when we talk about teaching, it's important to talk about the hard parts first, and not the other way around. I think too many teaching programs and books sell being an educator as an almost uniformly positive gig, like, "Teaching is the world's *best* career! As a teacher, you will change the world every single day! I love getting up and going to work in the morning!" and then they quickly whisper under their breath, like the fine print at the end of a radio commercial, "Sometimesitmaybeever-so-slightlychallenging." While I completely agree with all of those positive sentiments about teaching (and yes, I really do look forward to going to work in the morning), I find the practice of recruiting teachers with unbalanced information irresponsible, like telling someone that climbing Mount Kilimanjaro is basically like walking up a big hill.

That being said, in this chapter, I would still like to tell you about one of my best days as a teacher from my rookie years. I wrote it down a few days after it happened. I share it with you because I'm proud of this story, and because we *should* be sharing stories of triumph in education, especially considering the hurdles we face as educators and the hurdles our kids face. But I also share it with you because I hope you will find it empowering, especially if you are at that difficult and scary part of teaching when you're doubting if these kinds of days even exist.

If you're not a teacher yet, I tell you with 100 percent certainty that you will absolutely make a positive difference in the lives of children. You will have your heart broken by beauty. Teaching will make you happy-cry, whether you manage to save it until you get home and shut your door or whether, on the last day of school, you blubber in front of a class of thirty students who then rush to ambush you with hugs.

Write your stories down, even if nobody reads them but you. You'll need them one day.

The following is based on a letter I originally published on my blog in 2014. At the time I simply wanted to share a particularly good teaching day with my family and friends, but I think another part of me was aware—even if I wasn't—of the importance of preserving moments like this, the rare (at first), glimmering bits of teaching magic that I had begun to doubt were possible. Though I addressed this letter to my students on a day years ago, it feels like I was writing to every student I've ever had; like something I could have written this semester. In a time when there are forces at work making it hard to do our jobs well, we could all use the reminder that at its core, *teaching is magic.*

Dear Students from March 26, 2014,

Sometimes being a teacher is hard.

It's been particularly hard lately because we're in the middle of standardized testing season, which, as you know, turns us all into crazy people. Between my class and your other classes, you guys take six tests a week to see if you're ready for the battery of standardized tests coming up. When we're not testing, I have to "drill and kill" you as administrators breathe down my neck, because their bosses are breathing down their necks, because the state is breathing down the districts' necks, and so on. (There is a lot of neck-breathing going on.)

Anyway, all of my colleagues thought I was crazy for scheduling a poetry memorization project in the middle of testing season, and with good reason. You guys said I was crazy, too. Making you memorize poetry when you've got mountains of packets of test review? That's flirting with an Eighth Amendment violation, right there.

But I explained to you why we're doing this. I said that when we memorize poetry, we internalize it; we have a new relationship with it. When we learn a poem by memory, inexplicably, it becomes a part of us. We learn about tone, mood, enjambment, and sound devices, yes, but we also learn how much meaning can fit in a two-second pause. We learn about practice. We learn that not all learning can fit on a worksheet or a PowerPoint or a Google Doc. We learn that the walls of our comfort zones are at the exact height—not a centimeter higher—for us to step over them.

Today was the performance day, so I got to school extra early to decorate our room. As I stood on wobbly desks to hang Christmas lights from the ceiling tiles, it finally dawned on me that I was insane, and not because of the multiple fire/work safety rules I was violating.

I went to a bad place in my mind. I abandoned my faith in you.

I realized this assignment was going to be a disaster. I had asked too much of you. You are in seventh grade, after all. You most likely wouldn't be able to even appreciate the poem you'd chosen to memorize—many of you chose poets like Longfellow, Keats, and Byron, poets you don't usually read about until high school or college. Plus, some of you might not have someone at home who has the luxury of being able to put down everything they're doing to help you memorize it or the English proficiency to give you feedback as you practice.

And maybe the whole idea of this poetry project was just me being selfish. Was I unfairly projecting my nostalgia onto you because I did a poetry memorization project in fifth grade and loved it? Was this project outdated and stale? Surely better teachers than me would have their students Skyping with a class in Thailand to translate a poem or coding digital avatars to perform a poem for a virtual reading. (Never mind that we rarely have access to technology that actually works or doesn't take twenty minutes to log in and boot up, but still.)

I got down from the desk I was standing on and began to panic.

I had visions of what might happen when I called your name to perform. Maybe you would stammer out half of a stanza before bursting into tears. Maybe when I called your name you would call out from your desk apathetically, "I didn't learn mine." Maybe you would say your poem with zero emotion or flavor or pitch, negating every reason I had assigned the project. Maybe I would call your name only to find out you went home at lunch, sick from nerves.

I thought, I will let the first few kids go and see if I need to call the whole thing off.

I thought, Maybe I'll just take it as an extra credit grade.

I thought, What was I thinking?

I thought wrong. You blew me away.

One student memorized a nearly four-hundred-word spoken word poem that included a singing part. We had to scrape our jaws off the floor.

Another, a recent immigrant, left us breathless when she shared Langston Hughes's "Let America Be America Again."

There was the girl who is painfully shy in class. She will barely speak above a whisper to me, and doesn't speak at all to her classmates. In a clear, loud voice, she performed every single word of Amy Gerstler's "Touring the Doll Hospital" flawlessly, her words easily reaching the back row. You guys gave her a standing ovation. I don't know if you saw her while you were clapping, but she wasn't just smiling. She was laughing triumphantly, like I have done this brave thing.

Then there was our class goofball who didn't just perform but absolutely became "First Love," speaking with the kind of tenderness that I think would have melted John Clare had he been in the room with us. (In a way, I think he was.)

There were the courageous young men and women who wrote and memorized original poems about self-harm, bullying, and other deeply personal subjects, and their vulnerability moved us to tears. Others of you wrote and performed poems about hamburgers or monkeys with mustaches, and we laughed, because good poetry makes you laugh, too.

Sometimes I forget what it means to be a teacher. Sometimes I begin to feel like my job is answering e-mails, or making Excel spreadsheets with arbitrary numbers next to your names, or going to meetings where I hear about more e-mails and spreadsheets and numbers next to your names and reasons why we should be worried about you.

But other times you—your energy, your creativity, your grit, your aliveness—reach out and shake me by the shoulders. You remind me why I'm here, what my real job is. You remind me that your potential is not for me to question but to believe in and fight for and insist on, because it's there, always. You remind me that you don't need protecting from challenges, you just need me to stand beside you and maybe hand you equipment as you wrestle with them. You remind me that being on this planet and learning alongside you is my greatest privilege. You are constantly extending that invitation to me— helping me remember why I'm here—and I'm sorry for forgetting that.

Thank you for shaking me by the shoulders.

Metaphorically. (Please don't do it literally.)

Love,

Teach

Acknowledgments

I have so much gratitude for all the people and their collective time and energy that have made this project possible.

Huge thanks to Lucia Watson, Suzy Swartz, and the whole team at Avery. I couldn't have assembled better people to have in my corner for a project so close to my heart. Dream team, for real.

I needed one person to believe in me first, and a huge thank-you to Sharon Pelletier, who did just that.

Thank you to the wonderful faculty and literary community at Vermont College of Fine Arts, but especially to Cynthia Huntington, who made me believe I was a writer.

Thank you to all the wonderful teachers who read early drafts, contributed ideas, or have helped shape my thinking about what it means to be a teacher and a leader. This book is what it is because of Mitzi Mak, Lisa Treleaven, Catherine Perez, Melody Gerard, Lynda Maxwell, Patricia Kassir, Linda Alexander, Katie Wood-Sponsel, Jordan Rowe, Sarah Feese, and the entire faculty and staff of Spring Branch Academic Institute.

Thank you to Kristen Wiley and Jillian Donley for your photography contributions to this book. You are both brilliant camera wizards.

A big bear hug to Angel at EQ for keeping me encouraged and caffeinated over several years.

Thank you to friends who have loved me so well, and especially to Sadie Grzywa, Leslie Bell, Mallory Dean, and Ashlee Newton, the VIP section of my fan club and the closest thing I have to sisters. And to all my friends, whether I've met you, and whether you know me as Love, Teach or Kelly, your support and our shared community are why I'm still teaching. From the deepest, most resonant place in my heart: thank you.

I have such a grateful heart for my brothers, Andrew and Greg, who made me funny and fearless, and to my parents, Don and Jean, who taught me that leaders are kind above everything else. Thank you to my grandma Joan, the original lady boss. And to Gavin, my biggest (and tallest) fan. You are my home.

And finally, to my students. Thank you for always reminding me what a gift it is to watch you grow up; to read and write and learn with you. I'm so lucky. Teaching can be hard sometimes, but you have always been and continue to be the best part of my day. I hope you leave my class believing that you have everything inside of you to help build us a better world, whatever that might look like. Go do it.